Aʟᴀʀᴍ ɪs ᴇᴠᴇʀʏᴡʜᴇʀᴇ ᴅɪsᴘʟᴀʏᴇᴅ over signs of moral and spiritual poverty in our youth. Headlines on drug addiction among school children and dishonesty among collegiate athletes are bringing demands that the schools do something before it is too late. Realization grows that military power alone will not save a nation which becomes morally bankrupt.

For three years educators in Kentucky have conducted a program for developing moral and spiritual values in the public schools which would not involve an expensive new department and additional personnel or violate the historic principle of separation of church and state.

The guiding spirit in this movement is William Clayton Bower, one of the nation's outstanding philosophers of education. His book is a report on the Kentucky experiments and a guide to those who wish to set up their own program on a sound and practical basis.

Professor Bower's book is based on the idea that moral and spiritual values are intrinsic to the learning process. In the classroom and in all school activities situations rich in value potentials constantly occur. Teachers trained to recognize value aspects in learning situations can help young people to make these values a part of their lives.

The Kentucky program is a *program of emphasis*. It requires only that the teaching staff be made aware of the simple ways of recognizing moral and spiritual values as they occur in the learning process and of helping students to discover them.

Everyone concerned with this vital prob-

Moral and Spiritual Values
in Education

William Clayton Bower

Moral and Spiritual Values in Education

University of Kentucky Press

LEXINGTON

Preface

WHATEVER organizational forms human life may take beyond mid-point in the twentieth century, it is certain that moral and spiritual values must be given greater substance if that life is to be more satisfying and less terrifying than in 1951. Everyone agrees with this. We say that to bring a tougher fibre of integrity into the governmental fabric we need politicians who are more sensitive to moral and spiritual values. We say that to use our natural resources wisely, husbanding them for the future while at the same time sustaining the present, we need scientists and industrialists whose moral and spiritual predominate over their materialistic values. We say that if modern man is not to perish as he finds his new place in a global society, his moral and spiritual values need to discipline and direct his scientific skills so that good instead of evil may result from his creativity.

These are the things we say, most of us, until the saying is monotonous. It is as though repetition of the phrases will bring about the situation desired. But change does not come by wishing and affirmation alone. It is a process of slow constructing. The wish may well be father to the thought, and the thought may be the forerunner of the practice (although that this is always so is debatable, in the light of man's behavior) but it is the practice, sustained and made habit, that brings the wish and thought to birth in a new reality. And, pathetically, it is at the point of practice in moral and spiritual values that we have been so inept as to be almost criminal.

The practice of moral and spiritual values must be within the physical context of time and place. It is this that makes it hard to be moral and spiritual. We have tried, by denial, to obliterate the reality of the material context of spiritual values, but even the ascetic, perched at the end of his swaying pole, had to eat. We have set up a dual system, the material goods and "practical things" of life being one, and the moral and spiritual being the other, but that dualism led to and sustained the secular-sacred dichotomy that resulted in the emasculation of both.

There being no further alternative, we are now confronted by the necessity of finding moral and spiritual values within man's continuum of earthy experience, as he lives his life in the constant context of social, scientific, and human relationships. It is no wonder that man is only now ready seriously to explore this third alternative. It is harder than the others. How be spiritual while digging a foxhole? How be moral while working a problem of sanitary engineering? How, actually, "go the second mile" when the first is noisy with distress?

This book deals with this multiple problem at the most promising point—education in the public schools. The basic philosophy is summarized in the author's words as follows: "Morality and spirituality are qualities that are potentially inherent in any and every experience of growing persons in their interaction with their natural, social, cultural, and cosmic world rather than abstract 'traits.' Moral and spiritual values are, therefore, indigenous to the school community and the learning process, and are not to be injected into the school by some outside agency. Consequently, the procedure indicated is to help the pupils and teachers discover these values as they are being generated in the school experience, to identify them, to develop them with the resources available to the school, and to carry them through into action in actual school situations. . . . The program should be one of emphasis and integrated into the total program of the school, rather than one of adding new content, courses, or departments."

But this book doesn't stop with philosophy. The how, the where, and the when (these are the points beyond the glittering affirmations where most books stop) are dealt with at length. "The problem of moral and spiritual education is, therefore, twofold. On the one hand, it is to help pupils to experience these values by making choices that are moral and spiritual in their nature and carrying through their decisions from intention to action in specific and concrete situations. On the other hand, it is to help the pupils to build up their many specific decisions and actions into generalized attitudes toward all situations and into dependable patterns of behavior."

To these two basic problems the author brings a lifetime of courageous reflection and experience. To them he also brings, as case studies, the actual experiences of actual children and teachers in actual classrooms in Kentucky, where an experimental program of education in moral and spiritual values has been in process for the past several years.

This book cuts a wide swath through the tangled underbrush of church and state, religion and education, sacred and secular, spiritual and materialistic, "body and soul," and lets in a lot of light. Further, many educators will follow thankfully in the lighted path. Dr. Bower, in this volume, has become a major directive factor in American education for the next generation.

RAYMOND F. McLAIN
General Director, Commission on Christian Higher Education, National Council of Churches of Christ in the U. S. A.

Acknowledgments

THE AUTHOR wishes to thank the University of Chicago Press for permission to draw freely upon certain ideas which he earlier expressed in *Character through Creative Experience* and *Church and State in Education,* as well as other publishers from whose books quotations have been made. He wishes also to thank the Rev. William Robert Insko for the use in Section III of Chapter II of the findings of his research in the several types of program in the field of moral and spiritual values now being carried on in the public schools of the United States. His thanks are due likewise to Mr. Maurice Warner for drawing the figures. He acknowledges with gratitude his dependence upon the many and invaluable contributions made by the members of the workshops and the participants in the pilot experimental schools. In a real sense the philosophy and techniques reported and interpreted in this volume represent the collective judgment of the author, the staffs of the workshops, and the participating principals and teachers in the experimental schools.

WILLIAM CLAYTON BOWER

Contents

Introduction

A PRIME purpose of all education is good character.

The first schools in this country were established as the result of a religious conviction our Pilgrim Fathers brought with them: they believed that it was essential to know how to read the Scriptures to obtain eternal life. For a long time the Bible was the principal textbook.

During the eighteenth and nineteenth centuries, and reaching into the first decade of the twentieth century, the curriculum of our schools was heavily loaded with materials that emphasized moral and spiritual values. Bible readings, Aesop's fables, the McGuffey readers, carefully selected gems from literature which emphasized fundamental virtues—these became the core of instruction in reading, exerting a powerful influence on the lives of children. But with the passing of time, with greater emphasis on nationalism, and with the development of science, the content of the curriculum in the public schools was broadened, and gradually less emphasis was placed upon moral and spiritual values.

Some religious denominations and some groups with little interest in any religion have opposed religious instruction in the public schools. This culminated in 1947 in *People of State of Illinois* v. *Board of Education,* better known as the *McCollum Case,* which challenged the right of the public schools to co-operate in offering a program of religious instruction. The Supreme Court of the United States invalidated the program provided in the Illinois schools on the ground that it violated the Federal Constitution and the principle of separation of church and state.

This decision has caused considerable alarm on the part of many of our leading citizens. They point out that since no religious instruction can be offered in the public schools, the moral instruction of youth will be neglected. Many educators and religious leaders are endeavoring to find some means whereby the spiritual development of our youth may not be neglected in the public schools.

Dr. Bower has given us a penetrating analysis of the discovery of moral and spiritual values and of the methods by which youth is led to accept and appreciate these values and thereby pattern his behavior. His book is by far the finest guide for achieving a higher morality for all citizens of a democracy that I have thus far found in the literature of religion, ethics, sociology, or education.

Personally, I agree with the Supreme Court decision that in a democracy religion as such cannot be taught in the public schools. The religious instruction of children must be provided primarily by the home and the church, but an understanding and appreciation of moral and spiritual values by our youth *is* a fundamental objective of our schools. For a school to neglect to teach its children that wisdom, which is essential to a comprehension of the moral and spiritual values, is to fail its most important work.

Our generation is face to face with a moral crisis. The rise in Europe of dictators who have challenged all moral principles and spiritual values, disregarding the fundamental concepts of right and justice that have slowly emerged through the centuries, is a perfect example of this moral bankruptcy. Today in our own country the Kefauver and Fulbright investigations by Congress have revealed a shocking disregard of moral principles that we have always considered fundamental. The scandals in collegiate athletics, recently revealed, are further evidence of how far reaching is this disregard of the eternal truths of life. These happenings should be a warning to the nation that some action must be taken that will place greater emphasis on moral and spiritual values if our kind of civilization is to survive. We cannot depend entirely upon the church or home for the teaching of these values. Too many of our children do not attend church. Too many of our homes neglect to instruct their children in the cardinal virtues so important in life. To reach all of our children some program of moral and spiritual education must supplement the teachings of the home and the church.

The school is more than just the curriculum; it is a community in which occur countless situations potentially rich in moral and spiritual values. In all of our instruction we are dealing with moral and spiritual values. It is essential that the teacher understand this fact; it is important that he possess the skill and technique of helping our youth to discover and develop these values at the psychological moment.

In this volume Dr. Bower has presented an approach to this subject which, if followed by the classroom teacher, should result in a sound and enriching program of emphasis on the moral and spiritual values which all men must comprehend if they are to live the good life.

HERMAN LEE DONOVAN
President, University of Kentucky

PART ONE

The Educational Situation

The problem dealt with in this volume is the outgrowth of the development of American education in relation to changes in American culture. These changes set the problem of moral and spiritual values in education in its contemporary form and call for a new approach to it and a new solution.

CHAPTER ONE

The Problem

AMERICAN education can be understood only when viewed as a historical process, the evolving character of which is the result of the interaction of many social factors. During the somewhat more than three centuries of national history, it has undergone many and fundamental changes. At no time have these changes been more profound than since the beginning of the present century.

I

The basic characteristics of early American education were carried over from its European backgrounds. But with the development of the frontier and the occupation of a vast continent, with their attendant cultural changes and demands, American education assumed characteristically American form. Now that the vast natural frontier has ceased to exist, like American culture, it has turned inward upon itself and is facing a new frontier of social problems within the nation and arising out of our relation to other nations in an unprecedentedly complex and tense global situation. American education in the rapidly changing contemporary world is confronted by new problems and new demands which call for a re-examination of its basic philosophy, content, and procedure.

One fundamental and increasingly important change in American education has been the shift of emphasis away from values to knowledge, techniques, and the so-called useful subjects and skills. As a result, many persons have come to feel that the weakest point in education is at the level of values.

This defect has been raised to the point of extreme urgency by the present conflict of ideologies between totalitarianism and democracy. This is a conflict of ends as well as of means, and both in the final analysis rest upon antithetic systems of values. In the surging, massive social forces of our generation, democracy as a way of life—with its emphasis upon freedom, the worth of the individual person, and autonomy —is being put to its severest test: whether or not it can endure against the pressures of an aggressive, militant, and imperialistic totalitarian thrust toward world domination. Under such circumstances, democracy is being forced to reexamine its fundamental assumptions regarding the human ends it seeks and the means by which it would achieve them. And since this conflict is at base a conflict of values, the ground on which this mortal struggle must be waged is ultimately that of values.

As one who has given thought to the functional relation of education to a people's culture would expect, this defect in American education reflects a fundamental defect in American culture. As President Hoover's Commission on *Recent Social Trends* pointed out in 1933, the profile of American culture is seriously unbalanced. In the fields of science, technology, and industry there have been astonishing achievements. But in the area of values—morality, art, and religion— there has been a corresponding cultural lag. The Commission pointed out the urgency of restoring a proper balance between knowledge and techniques on the one hand and values on the other.

The Director of the study on Social Trends, Dr. William F. Ogburn, has also called attention to a shift in the functions of social institutions. For some time the family, the church, and the local community have been surrendering functions to industry, the school, and the state. Whether this realignment of functions is desirable or not, it may be noted that it not only places the school in a strategic position for interpreting and influencing culture, but lays upon it a correspondingly grave responsibility.

II

Emphasis on values was once an integral part of American education. The earliest schools in America were predominantly religious. This was especially true in New England and the Middle Colonies, the settlers of which had come to the newly discovered country in search of religious liberty. It was true also in the Southern Colonies, though the motivation for migration was different. In New England the compulsory public schools were administered by the clergy, and orthodoxy of religious belief was a primary qualification of teachers. The content consisted of the hornbook from which the Lord's Prayer was learned, the catechism, the Bible, and the New England Primer. In this Calvinistic theocracy church and state were united. In the Middle Colonies, however, the sectarianism of the settlers was so diverse that any common system of education was impossible. As a result, all education was parochial. In Virginia and the other Southern Colonies the motivation for migration was chiefly, though not exclusively, economic. Nevertheless, the Southern Colonists brought with them their Anglican form of life. In this aristocratic society, whether education was by private tutor, in schools in England, or in the charitable plantation schools, religion was universally assumed.

One of the greatest changes to take place in American education was its secularization. By the latter part of the nineteenth century, the exclusion of religion from the public schools was largely complete. Several factors contributed to this complex process. One was the geographical expansion of the frontier. In New England the life of the colonists, including education, centered in the town meeting, a religio-political unit. But as the population moved westward, the geographical unit supplanted the town meeting as the basis of the community. In time this led to the school district which was a political and secular, rather than a religious, unit.

Furthermore, as the life of the colonies developed as well as expanded, new functions emerged in the increasingly complex society. Boundary surveys, transportation, travel, commerce, communication—all these required knowledge and skills not provided for in the catechism and the New England Primer. Then, as now, these new demands upon education led to the introduction of additional secular content into the once almost exclusively religious curriculum.

But the principal factor which led to the secularization of American education was the sectarianism of American religion. The competition of the sects for the control of education made the separation of church and state a crucial issue, brought to a head by the insistence of the churches upon the division of public funds for ecclesiastical use. The struggle against this, under the leadership of Horace Mann, secretary of the Massachusetts Board of Education, was long and bitter. Eventually, in amendments to state constitutions, constitutions of newly admitted states, and court decisions, the division of public funds with ecclesiastical institutions and the teaching of sectarian religion in the public schools were prohibited, and the principle of the separation of church and state was formalized into a basic American doctrine. By 1875 the process of the legal and formal secularization of American education was virtually complete.

In the light of these historic facts, it is quite clear that the secularization of the public schools was due chiefly to sectarian competition and divisiveness, not to hostility to religion as such. Both Horace Mann and Thomas Jefferson were deeply religious men. Nevertheless, the practical result was the exclusion of religion from the schools. Even more significantly, the exclusion of religion from the schools accentuated still further the shift of emphasis from values to knowledge and techniques.

In addition to these specific factors contributing to the exclusion of religion from the schools, there has been a marked and steady tendency since the Renaissance toward the secularization of modern Western culture. It was inevitable that this trend should have a profound effect upon education which, as its history clearly demonstrates, reflects the orientation and temper of the contemporary culture.

III

Our generation is confronted by the long-term results of the secularization of education. In retrospect, this solution of the problem under the conditions existing in the nineteenth century appears to have been the best, if not the only, solution. Nevertheless, many of its consequences were neither foreseen nor intended. Since in America religion was, and to a large extent still is, identified with its sectarian theological beliefs and ecclesiastical structures, the prohibition of the teaching of the denominational expression of religion in the public schools led to the exclusion of religion itself, one of the most fundamental and universal forms of valuational experience.

Much has happened in recent years to change the situation in America since the public schools were secularized. One event has been a new and deeper understanding of the functional origin and nature of religion. Scientific, as distinguished from theological, study has resulted in a definite trend toward a functional concept of religion. In the light of anthropological, sociological, historical, and psychological research, religion is coming to be seen as man's oldest, most fundamental, and universal reaction to his objective world. It is as much a phase of his interaction with his world of reality as science, philosophy, technology, or the arts. As discussed in detail in Section IV of Chapter VI, it is essentially a revalued experience in which all particular values—economic, political, intellectual, esthetic, and moral—are integrated, fused, and heightened into a total meaning and worth of life in relation to ultimate reality. While specialized interests and activities tend to cause compartmentalization of life, religious revaluation leads toward the wholeness of life in relation to its total environment. Thus, religious beliefs and practices have their origin in the several areas of man's interaction with his natural, social, and cosmic world. They vary as the cultural interests and activities of the cultural group vary, and change within the same cultural group as its practical interests and activities change, as in the concept of God among the ancient Hebrews or such theological doctrines as the Atonement in Western civilization. Reciprocally, these integrated religious values re-enter the areas of specialized interests and activities as factors of criticism and reconstruction.

In the meantime, the issues, both social and theological, that gave rise to sectarianism largely have ceased to exist, and the sharp lines of demarcation between sects have undergone deterioration. In their place have come large-scale ecumenical movements, with their emphasis upon understanding and co-operation. At the same time, new social problems of unprecedented complexity and danger have arisen that challenge all the intellectual, moral, and spiritual resources of mankind. There is a growing conviction that these problems cannot be solved by scientific, technological, or diplomatic resources alone, but ultimately by dependence on moral and spiritual values.

Thus it becomes clear why the secularization of education in America has been followed by results that could not at the earlier time be foreseen and certainly were not intended. The exclusion of sectarianism from the schools was no loss. But the unintended exclusion of religion, which functionally conceived is the most profound and universal of all valuational experience, was an incalculable loss. Considered negatively, it removed the greatest deterrent to the shift of emphasis from values to knowledge and techniques. To put it positively, it removed the solid and rational basis for the achievement of a sustaining and effective system of functioning values necessary to a philosophy of life and to dynamic and creative personal and social living. The fundamental tragic consequence lay not in the fact that religion as conventionally and traditionally understood was eliminated from the schools, but in the fact that a vacuum was created in the entire realm of values.

Another consequence immediately following from the loss of the value content of education has been the tendency of personal and social experience to fall apart. The great periods of cultural synthesis have been those in which moral and spiritual values have been in the ascendancy. Modern devalued education and culture has tended toward specialization and compartmentalization. Particular interests and activities come to be pursued for their own limited and isolated ends, without reference to other interests and activities or to the whole of personal and social experience.

Still another consequence of the fragmentation of personal experience and culture has been the loss of the sense of the meaning and worth of life. This has resulted in the loss of a stable orientation of life toward ends of supreme worth, in confusion, in frustration, and in disillusionment and pessimism. The question, "What is life all about, anyway?" ultimately is followed by the devastating question, "What is the use?" The sense of personal isolation and the feeling of insecurity are among the most disintegrating emotions in their effect upon personality. Ours is a disillusioned generation, increasingly unsure of itself and depressed by a sense of inadequacy in the presence of increasingly urgent and difficult demands. This is why the cynical Aldous Huxley wrote his *Ends and Means,* in which he insists that the time has come for modern man to rediscover the values that are capable of giving meaning and worth to life and to subordinate techniques to them. This is why H. G. Wells, after he had published his *Outline of History* and his *Work,*

Wealth, and Happiness of Mankind, was impelled to write his *What Shall We Do with Our Lives?* in which he sets forth his conviction that the next immediate cultural task is to achieve a synthesis of modern life through the rediscovery of values and their organization into a rational, coherent, and functioning system, comparable to the historic periods of cultural synthesis through the historic religions.

This is the new problem that confronts education in America today. It is no longer the problem of churchmen desiring to have their interpretation of religion taught in the public schools or on released time. It has become a problem of the whole democratic community, in which educators, parents, statesmen, jurists, and social workers as well as churchmen are becoming concerned as citizens responsible for the future of democracy.

IV

There is indubitable evidence of a growing concern over this problem of moral and spiritual values in education. In 1932 the Department of Superintendence of the National Education Association devoted its annual Yearbook to *Character Education.* It said (p. 23) : "Our society today awaits a new integration of knowledge, aspiration, and human purpose which will take into account the findings of science, the theory of evolution, and the growing power of the laboring classes, as well as the influence of great spiritual leaders. Until such an integration is forthcoming, the present condition of moral chaos is likely to continue and the more fundamental problems of character education will defy solution. Whether this is the task of the church or some other agency we cannot say today; but it would seem to be a task that is essentially religious in nature."

There was no area of child and youth need to which the 1940 White House Conference on Children in a Democracy gave more concerned attention than to the problem of moral and spiritual values in education. After careful consideration of the problems involved, the Conference adopted the following recommendation (*Proceedings*, p. 31) : "Practical steps should be taken to make available to children and youth through education the resources of religion as an important factor in the democratic way of life and the development of personal and social integrity. To this end the Conference recommends that a critical and comprehensive study be made of the various experiences both of the churches and of the schools in dealing with the problem of religion in relation to public education. The purpose of such a study would be to discover how these phases of education may best be provided for in the total program of education, without in any way violating the principle of the separation of church and state."

In 1944 the John Dewey Society devoted its Seventh Yearbook to this problem under the title, *The Public Schools and Spiritual Values*. It not only expressed its unqualified conviction regarding the responsibility of the school for fostering spiritual values, but outlined a theoretical and practical basis for procedure. "It is this total situation of callous selfishness, undigested social change, disturbed culture, weakened authority of custom, social perplexity—with the resulting lessening of man's faith in himself—which calls so urgently upon us to uphold and strengthen our spiritual values. Indeed the essential quality of civilization itself seems herein at stake. The particular concern of this book is the public school and the part it can and should play in the support and defense of the spiritual values necessary to a desirable civilization. . . . Such a public service we of this book count the chief task and aim of the public school. It is to help the school discharge this particular spiritual task and duty that this book has been undertaken" (pp. 1-2).

In 1947 the American Council on Education appointed a commission to study this problem and to make recommen-

dations. The personnel of the commission consisted of outstanding leaders of American education, both public and
private. After an analysis of the problem, the commission
recommended in *The Relation of Religion to Public Education* in the most forthright way the inclusion of the study
(as distinguished from the teaching) of functional, non-
sectarian religion in the regular school curriculum, on the
same basis as the study of any other subject. "The problem
is how to find a way to give due recognition in public education to the place of religion in the culture and in the convictions of our people while at the same time safeguarding
the separation of church and state. A solution, as we see it,
requires the charting of a middle course between the existing
situation and the adoption of experiments which are un-
warranted. The exclusion of religion from the public schools
which so largely prevails today results in its relegation in
the minds of youth to a position of relative unimportance.
This runs counter, we believe, to the intention of the American school system from the beginning. On the other hand,
any educational innovation which would tend to identify
public education with a particular body of sectarian beliefs
and practices we hold to be not only impracticable but im-
proper" (p. 49).

This mounting concern is further evidenced by the fact
that the topic given highest priority in the work of the
Educational Policies Commission for 1950 was Moral and
Spiritual Values in Education. In its *Moral and Spiritual
Values in the Public Schools,* the Commission said (pp. 3, 4,
55) : "The American people have rightly expected the schools
of this country to teach moral and spiritual values. The
schools have accepted this responsibility. The men and
women who teach in these schools, as responsible members
of society, share its system of values. As educators, they are
engaged in a vocation that gives a central place to values as
guides to conduct. . . . No society can survive without a
moral order. A system of moral and spiritual values is in-

dispensable to group living. As social structures become more complex, as the welfare of all depends increasingly upon the co-operation of all, the need for common moral principles becomes more imperative. Especially in a society which cherishes the greatest possible degree of individual freedom, the allegiance of the individual to commonly approved moral standards is necessary. No social invention however ingenious, no improvements in government structure however prudent, no enactment of statutes and ordinances however lofty their aims, can produce a good and secure society if personal integrity, honesty, and self-discipline are lacking. . . . Since the ultimate success of a program to develop moral and spiritual values depends largely on the teacher, the institutions which educate teachers should give full recognition to these values in their curricula. . . . School administrators, having placed an emphasis on character in the selection process, should encourage teachers to use initiative and imagination in the development of their subject matter in ways which teach moral and spiritual values."

These verbal statements by national educational bodies, to say nothing of innumerable expressions by outstanding individual leaders and organizations, evidence a vivid awareness of the problem and an urgency to do something about it. To them must be added an increasing number of experiments on the part of local and state school systems in programs of moral and spiritual education. Professor Clarence P. Shedd's survey has revealed that 60 per cent of state institutions of higher learning are experimenting with programs of one sort or another in introducing religion into their curricula.

This evidence can mean only one thing: that sensitive Americans are becoming aware of the disastrous consequences of the neglect of moral and spiritual values in education and are ready to re-examine the problem in its new aspects and to search for a constructive solution with all the resources at their command.

CHAPTER TWO

Toward A Solution

THE MAIN outlines of the problem arising from the neglect
of moral and spiritual values in American education are
quite clear, but the solution of the problem is anything but
clear. It involves the nature and ends of education, the
origin and nature of moral judgments and spiritual attitudes,
and the interrelated functions and responsibilities of church
and state in a democratic society.

Moreover, the problem has not remained the same. American culture has passed through many changes since the
thirteen colonies were founded on the eastern seaboard. The
development of the frontier and its later disappearance, the
vast tides of immigration from Europe with their diverse
racial stocks and cultural traditions, the growth of a vast
industrial potential, the involvement and unsought leadership of America in international affairs—these are some of
the factors that have produced these changes. New demands
upon education have arisen out of these altered conditions
now that the nation is thrust into the midst of the massive
social and political forces of a global society torn asunder
by an apparently mortal conflict between totalitarian armed
aggression and the democratic way of life. In this changed
social situation the problem of moral and spiritual values is
not the same as it was a century ago, nor can the solution be
the same.

I

The earliest approach to the problem of moral and spiritual values in a secularized education was made by the
churches. When upon the exclusion of religion the public

school assumed responsibility for secular education, the churches undertook to offer religious education. They adopted the Sunday school, a philanthropic institution imported from England in the latter part of the eighteenth century. Pietistic and evangelistic, it met for an hour on Sunday, was taught by untrained laymen, and had for its subject matter an exclusively biblical content fragmentarily selected.

By the beginning of the twentieth century educational ideals and methods began to influence the Sunday school. In 1908 graded lessons with considerable extrabiblical material were adopted by the more progressive churches. In 1922 forty of the principal denominations, representing approximately 85 per cent of the Protestants of the United States and Canada, joined their educational forces to form the International Council of Religious Education. This organization, under a highly trained professional staff, has developed an educational program of great merit.

At the same time the parochial type of education originating in the Middle Colonies was carried on by some of the larger churches, notably the Roman Catholic and the Lutheran. These parochial schools undertook to teach the children of their members both religious and secular subjects at their own expense. The same intense interest in the religious content of education and protest against the secularism of the public schools led other communions, especially the Presbyterian and the Jewish, at one time or another to consider adopting the parochial system.

The outcome of this situation was the development of two separate systems of education. Public education evolved along scientific lines, with an elaborate philosophy, procedure, and organization, for all the young people of the nation. The Sunday school and the parochial school developed along pietistic and evangelistic lines for the children of the several denominations, leaving unreached more than half of the nation's juvenile population.

Meantime, a group of educators and churchmen, deploring the division of education into the secular and the religious, began to explore the possibility of integrating the two types of education. In 1903, under the leadership of President William Rainey Harper of the University of Chicago, this group organized the Religious Education Association for the purpose of introducing educational ideals into religion and religious ideals into education. An interfaith organization, this body has sought to provide an open forum through discussion and publication for the study of the interrelated problems of education and religion. Its achievement of this end has been considerable.

In somewhat the same mood, an experiment in integrating the two phases of education took the form of religious instruction given by the churches on time released, on the request of the parents, from the public school schedule. This was inaugurated in 1913 by a proposal of Superintendent William A. Wirt of the Gary, Indiana, public schools to the Gary churches that they offer religious instruction by church teachers, at the expense of the churches, and in church property on time released from the public school schedule under a unit of cultural subjects and activities in the school program. At first such instruction was offered by individual denominations, but later was offered co-operatively by a Community Council of Religious Education. This movement, known as Weekday Religious Education, spread rapidly throughout the nation, especially in the larger urban centers. It is now sponsored not only by the major denominations, but by a department of the International Council of Religious Education, now merged with the National Council of the Churches of Christ in the U.S.A. Weekday schools now are operating in some 3,000 communities in 46 states, with an enrollment of more than 2,000,000 children. Twenty-one of the 38 cities of America with more than a quarter million population have such programs. In some communities, as in Ohio and Virginia, religious instruction has been correlated with that of the public school.

As an experiment in establishing some working relation between secular and religious education the Weekday movement is significant. But that it is a solution of the fundamental problem not even its most ardent advocates would affirm. Aside from the fact that it does not reach the total child and youth population of the nation, it still leaves the value system (as represented by religion) and the knowledge and technique system all but dissociated.

In March of 1948 the Supreme Court in an 8-to-1 decision declared illegal the practice of giving religious instruction on released time in public school buildings in Champaign, Illinois. This ruling was aimed at the use by the churches of public school property and machinery rather than at the principle of released time as such. Nevertheless, it has raised certain additional questions about the adequacy of relying upon the churches for the primary responsibility for moral and spiritual values in the public school, particularly at the point where church and state impinge upon each other as institutions.

II

There are several variously sponsored community agencies of a private or semipublic nature that place great emphasis upon character development. Such are the Boy Scouts, the Girl Scouts, the 4-H Clubs, the Future Farmers of America, and the Future Homemakers of America. The Scouts derive their patterns of activities and symbols from outdoor contact with nature and primitive pioneer conditions. The last three base their programs on vocational interests, and in an effective way unite moral and spiritual ideals with the continuing interests and activities of mature life. For this reason they are particularly powerful in intrinsic motivation, so necessary in character development and so often lacking in most verbal and formal approaches. Nevertheless, these programs are confined to limited memberships and are more or less unrelated in their objectives and programs. Neither are they co-ordinated with the public school in a comprehensive program of education.

There are also a number of semiecclesiastical organizations working in one way or another with schools and state institutions of higher learning. Foremost among these are the Young Men's Christian Association, and the Young Women's Christian Association, and the Hi-Y clubs.

All these agencies, both public and private, are contributing much, each in its own way, to an emphasis upon moral and spiritual values (in other than the traditional or theological sense) in the experience of young people. Nevertheless, it remains true that these programs are not integrated into the total educational program of the school. Great as their contributions have been, the fundamental problem of moral and spiritual values in education has not been resolved. Nor can it be resolved by agencies outside the school. It is as much the responsibility of the school to develop moral and spiritual values in the nation's children and young people as it is to give them knowledge, the tools of learning, or the techniques of living. This responsibility inheres in the education of the whole person in his interaction with the total cultural tradition and the contemporary world. It is a responsibility which the school cannot legitimately delegate to any outside agencies, whatever their responsibility to develop these values may be in their own respective fields.

III

An inquiry addressed to the state superintendents of instruction gives a fair over-all picture of the emphasis which the several states are placing upon moral and spiritual values in education. No doubt there are localities in which something is being done in this phase of education that this survey did not bring to light because the activities are not known to the state departments of education or are not integral parts of their programs.[1]

Sixteen states and the District of Columbia report that they have no plans under way or in immediate contemplation to develop moral and spiritual values systematically in the schools. These include Arizona, Georgia, Illinois, Indiana, Missouri, Nebraska, New Mexico, New Jersey, North Carolina, North Dakota, Oregon, South Dakota, South Carolina, Minnesota, Montana, and West Virginia.

Four states—Virginia, California, Alabama, and Arkansas—while reporting no formal state-wide programs, express deep conviction about the place of moral and spiritual values in education and hope that their schools are accomplishing results in this area through their regular programs. Fairfax County in Virginia has developed a program for Instruction in Christian Principles of Living and the Major Religions of the World. Los Angeles, California, has a specific program under the title, "Moral and Spiritual Values in Education," and a State Committee is engaged in a thorough study of this problem. Alabama expresses the conviction that "the development of values is in a sense the woof of good education. All aspects of an educational program should contribute to such values." Arkansas feels that "the development of moral and spiritual values in education . . . involves the total school program and all the experiences that children and youth have under the school's direction."

Eighteen states have more or less specific programs for the development of moral and spiritual values, which fall under eight general types:

[1] William Robert Insko, "Report of Inquiry Regarding Emphasis of State Departments of Education upon Moral and Spiritual Values in the Public Schools" (unpublished manuscript). The data in this section are taken from this report.

1. *Good Citizenship.* Colorado, Connecticut, Delaware, Florida, Michigan, and Oklahoma are using this approach, with elaborate programs worked out in Connecticut, Florida, and Michigan.

2. *Temperance Education,* in Colorado, New Hampshire, and Mississippi.

3. *Released Time,* in Ohio, Pennsylvania, New York, and Maine.

4. *Mental Health,* in Louisiana, which has an elaborate program.

5. *Bible Reading,* especially in Idaho which has worked out a detailed schedule of readings selected from prose and poetry, orations and addresses, great prayers, songs and lyrics, words of wisdom, life of Jesus, miracles of the Old and New Testaments, parables, letters, and narratives.

6. *Character Education,* both "direct" and "indirect," especially emphasized in Massachusetts, Nevada, and Vermont. These programs follow the general pattern much in vogue in the thirties.

7. *Guidance.* Many schools in New Hampshire are attempting to develop attitudes and ideals through group guidance. In Louisiana several specially designed activities are outlined for providing rich and varied learning experiences for meeting the developmental needs of pupils. Outstanding among guidance programs is the National Forum Guidance Series, produced by the National Forum of Chicago with the aid of a large group of distinguished advisors and consultants. The series, designed for junior and senior high school students, includes: *Discovering Myself, Planning My Future, Toward Adult Living, Being Teen-Agers, High School Life,* and *About Growing Up.* The Students' Books are accompanied by Teachers' Guides and Visual Charts.

8. *Values Inherent in the Educational Process.* Maryland at an educational conference in 1949 attempted to identify the "ethical, moral, and spiritual values" which should re-

sult from the normal educational process and in 1950 began working out evaluative criteria and scales for translating these values into the conduct of administrators, teachers, and pupils. The Kentucky program as interpreted in this volume falls under this category.

Nine state superintendents did not respond to the inquiry, from which it may be inferred that little or nothing is being done in this phase of education in their states.

Speaking broadly, it may be said that as far as state programs are involved, there is a widespread concern about moral and spiritual values in education, that slightly less than half of the states are attempting to do something in solving the problem, and that in some eight or ten states well-considered programs of varying types are under way.

IV

In the light of these attempts it now seems clear that the solution of the problem of restoring moral and spiritual values in education must be sought in the school community itself and in the content and procedure of the educative process, by school personnel, with resources available to the school, and as an integral part of the total school program. This is the basic idea that underlies the experiment in the State of Kentucky and gives it such distinctive character as it may possess.

The Kentucky Program for the Discovery and Development of Moral and Spiritual Values in Education grew out of the concern of educators, parents, and lay leaders over the neglect of moral and spiritual values in the school program, and an urgent desire to do something about it. In 1946 the State Department of Education appointed a committee, composed of educators and laymen under the chairmanship of J. Mansir Tydings, to explore the problem and recommend procedures. In 1948 an Advisory Committee consisting of professional educators was created to counsel with the parent committee on principles, policies, and procedures. In October of 1948 a state-wide conference of superintendents, teachers, and heads of the teacher-education institutions of the state was held at the University of Kentucky upon the joint invitation of Boswell B. Hodgkin, Superintendent of Public Instruction, and Dr. Herman L. Donovan, President of the University of Kentucky. At this conference a statement of basic philosophy was unanimously adopted, and steps of procedure were outlined. These steps included the selection of six pilot experimental schools by the Department of Education in co-operation with the six sponsoring institutions—the University of Kentucky, the University of Louisville, Murray State College, Western Kentucky State College, Eastern Kentucky State College, and Morehead State College—the holding of a workshop at the University of Kentucky in June of 1949, and the beginning of experimental work in the pilot schools in the autumn of 1949.

The basic philosophy and techniques are outlined in Sections II and III of this volume.

The first workshop sought to prepare the participating teachers from the pilot schools for the experimentation. In addition to a general course on basic philosophy, four simultaneous project groups, under specialists, explored four areas of school experience: (1) an analysis of the relations, activities, and behavior situations of the school community; (2) an analysis of the content of the school curriculum; (3) helping pupils to meet adjustment situations through personal and group counseling; and (4) an analysis of the value potentials of physical education, sports, and recreation. A fifth group worked on the symbolic expression of moral and spiritual values through art forms, ceremonials, and celebrations.

The second workshop, held at the University of Kentucky in June of 1950, undertook to bring together the experience of the experimental pilot schools, to interpret and appraise it, and out of this process to produce resource materials for use in other schools. It was not intended to produce textbooks or to set up stereotyped procedures, but to give descriptions of a wide range of school experience in the five project areas, of what was done in each case, and of the changed attitudes of pupils and teachers, together with published resources. It is hoped that these results will stimulate other schools and teachers to work out their own programs creatively in the light of their own specific situations.

At the time this is written, the movement has passed through its first stage of exploration, formulation, and experimentation. The initial results are being incorporated into the Department of Education's *Curriculum Guide* for elementary and secondary schools and into the regular program for teachers in preparation in the tax-supported teacher-education institutions of Kentucky. A generous grant by the Lily Endowment has made it possible for Mr. Tydings to devote half of his time to the field supervision of the movement as a member of the staff of the Department of Education.

While this program is of the school, for the school, and by the school, it is in no sense in competition with or a substitute for religious education as given by the various churches for their memberships in terms of their several theological interpretations or ecclesiastical organizations of religion.

PART TWO

A Basic Philosophy

If any program is to be intelligent and productive of constructive and important results, it must be based upon and guided by ideas. In this section is set forth the basic philosophy of the Kentucky Program of Moral and Spiritual Values in Education.

CHAPTER THREE

Separation of Church and State

As suggested in Chapter I, the divisive influence of sectarianism and the competition of rival ecclesiastical bodies to control public education led to the adoption of the basic doctrine of the separation of church and state in education. While the earliest solution was aimed at the exclusion of sectarianism from the schools, its practical result was the exclusion of religion in its nontheological and nonecclesiastical form.

Now that a new and widespread concern has arisen over the restoring of moral and spiritual values to education, the issue between church and state has again become a live one. Is the responsibility for developing moral and spiritual values to be allocated to the churches as their exclusive prerogative? Or is the school as the chief interpreter of a people's culture to its young as much responsible for the cultivation of moral and spiritual values as it is for knowledge, skills, and the techniques of citizenship? If the churches are to assume responsibility for the introduction of moral and spiritual values into the public school program, how can they do this without violating at essential points the principle of the separation of church and state? If the school takes charge of the development of moral and spiritual values, can it do so without the encumbrance of theological interpretations or ecclesiastical complications? These are fundamental questions that must be answered in the context of American democracy before any satisfactory and workable philosophy for a program of moral and spiritual values can be arrived at.

I

Perhaps the most fruitful approach to an understanding of the contemporary problem of the separation of church and state in education will be to consider the specific points of tension that have arisen between the two institutions.

As the National Education Association has pointed out (*Research Bulletin,* XXIV, no. 1), the problem has exhibited three phases: (1) the elimination of church control over public schools; (2) the introduction of religious doctrine into the program; and (3) efforts to obtain aid from public sources for sectarian schools. The first of these largely was settled in the nineteenth century. The last two are currently live issues whose outcomes are far from being resolved.

One area of tension between church and state in education concerns aid to sectarian schools. Direct aid through tax levy or appropriations for sectarian schools is prohibited by constitutional provisions. But it is in the matter of indirect aid that conflict has arisen and has become the subject of legislative action or court decision. Numerous legal rulings have been made in each of these phases, but there is a considerable body of state legislation and practice that has not come under the review of the courts.

One aspect of tension in this area deals with the use of church buildings by the public school or with the use of school buildings by the churches. Of ten cases reviewed, three state courts held such use to be unconstitutional and seven held it to be permissible. A second aspect in this area involves furnishing free textbooks to parochial schools. The court of New York declared the practice illegal, while the courts of Louisiana and Mississippi ruled it legal, and an appeal of the Louisiana decision to the Supreme Court was upheld. The favorable decision was based upon a child benefit theory rather than upon aid to parochial schools.

Five states furnish textbooks and 44 states and territories do not. A third aspect in this area has to do with furnishing free transportation to pupils in parochial schools. The Maryland and New Jersey courts have approved this procedure, while courts in six other states have declared it illegal. Nineteen states and territories furnish free transportation, while 30 do not. Favorable court decisions rest in part upon the child benefit theory, but others upon the police responsibility of the state in providing public safety.

A second area of tension between church and state in education concerns the teaching of religion in the public school by the churches. This also has three aspects.

One aspect involves the employment of teachers wearing a distinctive religious garb, on the ground that, apart from specific courses in the religion of a sect, the wearing of such a habit exerts an indirect influence upon pupils. The courts of Pennsylvania, New York, and North Dakota have ruled that the wearing of a religious garb is not illegal, though Pennsylvania and New York subsequently have prohibited it, as have Arizona, Nebraska, and Oregon. In 1946, sixteen states and territories permitted the practice, and 22 prohibited it, the rest being noncommittal.

The second aspect in this area concerns the holding of religious exercises and the reading of the Bible as part of the public school program. Most of the courts that have reviewed the reading of the Bible have declared it legal, provided it is read without comment or sectarian interpretation and pupils are not required to participate. Exceptions have been Illinois, Louisiana, and South Dakota, where it was held that the religious freedom of Jews and non-Christians was thereby violated. Practice varies widely. Thirteen states and territories require Bible reading, 25 permit it, and 8 prohibit it. Practice concerning opening religious exercises, which usually include the reading of the Bible, the Lord's Prayer, and the singing of hymns, follows quite closely that of Bible reading. It was ruled illegal in Louisiana on the ground that it discriminated against the Jews (in the case of the New Testament), and in Nebraska, Pennsylvania, and Illinois either because the hymns were definitely denominational or Protestant, or because pupils were not excused from participation.

The third and sharpest current issue in this area involves the nation-wide practice of released time from the public school schedule for religious instruction given by church teachers either in church property or in public school buildings and with or without public school credit. Before the recent Supreme Court decision in the Champaign, Illinois, case, 35 states were excusing pupils for religious instruction by church teachers in church buildings, and the rest were not. Nearly a quarter of a century ago the New York court ruled in the Mount Vernon case that the practice was illegal on the ground that it violated the compulsory attendance law and misused public funds for the purpose of printing records. Two years later the court gave a somewhat contradictory opinion in the White Plains case, where record cards were furnished by the churches. By 1946, notwithstanding the fact that a number of states have enacted laws permitting this form of released time and local school boards have approved the plan in many communities, the New York case was the only one reviewed by the courts. In the form of released time in which the religious instruction is given by church teachers in public school buildings, the situation is quite different. The decision of the Circuit Court in the Champaign case upholding the practice was appealed to the Supreme Court, and that court by an 8-to-1 vote declared the practice unconstitutional. In addition to the one dissenting vote, however, four of the justices were unwilling to disapprove all religious education programs held on released time. This gave a balance of opinion in favor of released time where public school buildings are not used. It may be assumed that the objection may also include public school credit for courses offered by churches on released time.

A third area of tension between church and state in education concerns state supervision of parochial schools. This tension arises around such items as taxation, incorporation, curriculum, certification of teachers, compulsory attendance, health regulations, equipment, registration, and length of school term. These are judged by the state to be areas in which the state must insist upon universal standards in the interests both of the children for whom in the final analysis the state is responsible and of society for citizenship in which education is a primary instrument. Beyond these minimal essentials in the interests of child and public welfare the state does not attempt to impose any restrictions upon the range or content of the religious instruction offered. Nevertheless, within this general framework of public policy there is wide variation in practice. Twenty states and territories require equivalent terms; 18 do not. Fifteen require certification of teachers in parochial schools; 21 do not. Fourteen require registration with the state department; 20 do not. Nineteen require state approval of the courses of study; 18 do not. Twenty-two require the teaching of all or part of the United States constitution, American history, civics, physiology, and hygiene; 14 require none of these subjects. Fifteen require standards of facilities and equipment; 16 do not. Twenty-seven require the filing of attendance records; 14 do not. It is provided in most state constitutions that church properties are exempt from taxation on the ground that they are beneficial to the advancement of civilization and public welfare, though an Indiana court has held that tax exemption is essentially a state subsidy and imposes upon the taxpayer the involuntary support of religious institutions. Except for Virginia, West Virginia, and Missouri, the incorporation of religious institutions by the state is not considered a violation of separation of church and state.

II

These tensions arise from the fact that church and state have overlapping functions in a comprehending social community. Their complete separation is neither possible nor desirable. In man's associated life the community is the ultimate social reality. Both church and state are rooted in and dependent upon that reality, and, in the last resort, are accountable to that community for the service they render to it.

The interdependence of functions is immediately obvious upon consideration of the commonplace activities of the total community. Our coinage bears the inscription, "In God We Trust." Public officials take their oath of office upon the Bible. The Congress opens its sessions with prayer by an officially appointed chaplain. The Army, Navy, and Air Force regard the chaplaincy as one of their most important units, and the chaplains wear the United States military uniforms and are assigned military rank. Most governmental executives, legislators, and judges are churchmen whose religious attitudes and convictions have profound influence upon their conduct as functionaries of government. Presidents, governors, and mayors issue Thanksgiving proclamations, designate days of prayer in emergencies, and set days of special community religious observances. The government has used churches as morale builders in times of national stress.

On the other hand, religious groups engage in activities designed to influence legislative and political policy. Certain religious bodies have maintained lobbies in the national capital. Undoubtedly the defeat of Alfred E. Smith for the presidency was due largely to Protestant opposition. The enactment of the Prohibition Amendment was largely the result of the powerful sentiment of religious groups. The United States government has a representative with ambassadorial rank at the Vatican. Social action commissions and programs of the leading denominations are designed to arouse and guide the positive participation of church members in social policies and programs involving political action, either through church blocs or the individual action of church members as citizens.

The location of the conflict of church and state is not, therefore, at the functional, but at the structural level of the two institutions. The conflict arises out of the attempt of one of the institutions to control the other. Historically, this has led to the totalitarianism of the church, as in the Middle Ages, or of the state, as in Nazi Germany or Soviet Russia.

The recognition of this distinction between levels of function and of institutional structure suggests the direction in which the resolution of the conflict may be sought. That direction lies in the full recognition of the primacy of community over both church and state and the mutual responsibility of both to the community as the ultimate social reality. In their efforts to meet the needs of the community, both "secular" and "spiritual," their functions should and will inseparably intermingle, while their institutional structures will remain separate, as do the separate organs in the human body.

This calls for the wholehearted co-operation of church and state in meeting the needs of the total comprehending community as mutually free institutions in a free society. This is the fundamental and creative conception that underlies the historic American doctrine of the separation of church and state.

III

When this theory is translated into practice in the field of American education, it means the complete separation of church and state on the institutional level and at the same time understanding and wholehearted co-operation on the functional level in a shared attempt to meet the needs of children and young people in the total community. While maintaining the integrity of each institution, there needs to be a mutual understanding and division of labor.

In such a frankly recognized division of labor, there are certain things that the school as a public instrument of democracy can do in cultivating moral and spiritual values that no religious sect can do, while at the same time there are things that the religious sect can do that the school cannot and should not attempt to do.

It may fairly be said that the school is the most authentic interpreter of a people's culture. Through it society consciously and intentionally attempts to transmit to its young the cultural heritage of the past and to shape the attitudes and behaviors of its future citizens, while equipping them with the knowledge, techniques, and ideals essential to effective citizenship in a democracy.

On the basis of any objective judgment, one of the most important elements of the cultural heritage consists of its moral values and spiritual insights that have grown out of the millenia of man's interaction with his natural, social, and cosmic world as these are preserved in the great cultural traditions—literature, history, philosophy, science, religion, and art. These traditions constitute the subject matter of the school curriculum. To delete these values from the basic subject matter of the school is not only to distort the cultural heritage, but to falsify it. To neglect these values in helping the young to make an effective adjustment to the demands of the contemporary world is to deprive them of one of the most essential resources for personal and social living. This does not mean that these values are to be dragged in or moralized upon in the teaching of literature, history, the natural and social sciences, mathematics, or the arts. They are integral elements of these subject matters and should be dealt with openly, objectively, and naturally as they occur on the same basis as all other subject-matter content.

Precisely the same is true of the behavior situations that arise out of the many-sided relations and activities of the school community, involving the relations of person-to-person, person-to-group, and group-to-group. These are among the most educative influences of the school, perhaps exceeding those of formal learning. These social relations and functions are in their deepest nature moral and spiritual, and are the primary source from which moral standards and spiritual sensitivity arise. For this reason the school community is, par excellence, a laboratory for analyzing and interpreting these situations and carrying decisions through to action under mature guidance.

Whatever other social institutions, such as the family and the church, may do in cultivating moral and spiritual values, the school as the interpreter of culture to all children and young people and the primary instrument for the preparation for citizenship cannot evade its fundamental responsibility in the realm of values.

On the other hand, there are many things which the church can do in the cultivation of values that the school cannot and should not attempt to do. The churches, which in America are divided into more than 200 sects, interpret moral and spiritual values in terms of their several theological presuppositions. This they have a perfect right to do as private institutions under the provisions of religious freedom in America. Into these theological interpretations the school has no business to enter, just as a particular church has no right to impose its theological interpretations upon the school.

Moreover, each religious sect has its own particular membership which, while constituting only a segment of the total community, is bound together by common beliefs and enterprises into a sustained and sustaining fellowship. This fellowship is oriented toward an organized set of distinctly religious values. Membership is based upon the voluntary acceptance of a more or less formal creed and entered upon through a formal initiatory rite. Its end, in Protestant and Catholic churches, is salvation from sin through grace by faith in a divine Redeemer and achievement of personal immortality through identification with the Risen Lord. Its fellowship is deepened and vivified through participation in the sacrament of the Eucharist, while in Judaism the religious ends are fulfilled through covenant relations with God, mediated through an elaborate system of ceremonials. Religious truth is arrived at through supernatural revelation and is generally held to be authoritative. The sacraments are channels of supernatural grace administered by an ordained clergy. The church is regarded by Protestants and Catholics alike as of a supernatural nature and as the mystical body of Christ. The religious sect is characterized by techniques for self-examination, repentance for sin, and rededication. It is rich in the symbolism of redemption. These general and over-all characteristics vary with individual religious bodies from those that are conservative and fundamentalist to those that are liberal and modernist. In any case, however rigidly formulated or tenaciously held, these are the concerns of private and voluntary associations. Together, the membership of all sects and faiths comprises only slightly more than half of the population of the United States. Their religious educational programs reach slightly less than half of the child and youth population of the nation. These specific theological and ecclesiastical ends are beyond the purview of the school as a public instrument serving all the child and youth population of the nation. The school is neither constituted nor equipped to carry on these functions, just as the history of the educational efforts of the churches has abundantly demonstrated that they are not constituted or equipped to carry the responsibility of a total educational program in a democracy.

In the light, therefore, not only of the historic doctrine of the separation of church and state, but of the effective functioning of each in American society, there should be a complete separation of church and state as institutions, with frankly recognized division of responsibility in the field of education. It is the responsibility of the public school to develop moral and spiritual values as they occur in the relations and functions of the school community, the content of the curriculum, and its guidance program. It is the responsibility of the several private religious bodies to interpret moral and spiritual values in terms of their particular theological and ecclesiastical presuppositions, to initiate their young into their particular traditions, and to employ in ways they deem proper their particular disciplines of the religious life. In no sense should one be thought of as a substitute for or in competition with the other. By such a strict separation at the institutional level of church and state, the points of tension will be reduced to a minimum and each, freed from the temptation to control or exploit the other, will find the ground for a rich experience of understanding and cooperation in meeting the needs of growing persons and of society in a democracy.

CHAPTER FOUR

Personality and How It Develops

EDUCATION as modernly conceived has a twofold function, each inseparably related to the other. From the individual point of view, it is concerned with the fullest possible development of the whole person. From the social point of view, it involves the promotion of understandings regarding the social relations in which the growing person is involved, attitudes of co-operation, techniques of effective social participation, and citizenship.

A program of moral and spiritual values within this larger framework of education is concerned with the development of a certain quality of person whose attitudes and behaviors are inspired and controlled by moral and spiritual ideals, and with a society in which are united freedom and corporateness, rights and responsibilities, justice and brotherhood. Since personality is primarily a social product, and society is composed of individual persons whose character collectively determines the integrity of the group, these two objectives of education cannot be separated. Neither exists without the other.

Moreover, values are always the affairs of persons, both as individuals and in association. At the level of experience they are never abstract. They grow out of experience and they function in experience by giving it criteria for judging it, motivation, and direction.

Such considerations as these determine the approach to an understanding of the process by which moral and spiritual values may be developed. Such an understanding must begin with an insight into the nature of personality and the way by which it is realized.

I

In the light of modern biological, psychological, and sociological research, personality is to be conceived as a more or less stable organization of physico-chemical elements, reflexes, impulses, habits, ideas, attitudes, and purposes, undergoing continuous change.

While for the purpose of analysis and description these various elements of personality may be differentiated, in the living person they occur as a functioning whole. It is no longer possible, as the older psychology and theology supposed, to separate the human person into "body" and "soul" or into the "natural" and "spiritual" as distinct entities. The physical, mental, and spiritual, while distinguishable as phases or modes of personality, are so interdependent and inseparable that it is impossible to determine the boundary where one leaves off and the other begins. As is now well known, the human capacity to think and form purposes is dependent upon a physical structure—the elaborately developed cortex which exists only in elementary form in the lower animals. The endocrine glands play an immensely important part in the formation of personality. Lesions in the nerve and brain tissues destroy the competence of thought or moral judgment. The I.Q. definitely is set by the physical structure of the brain. On the other hand, mental and emotional states profoundly affect the functioning of the physical organism, as in the effect of morale upon the physical performance of the athlete or the soldier, even to the dramatic extent of inducing functional blindness or paralysis.

Moreover, the findings of modern science have revolutionized the once-obvious conception of matter, so that what formerly appeared as solid substance is, with deeper insight, seen to be nothing but organized energy, as open in texture as the stellar universe. This new understanding has led such a scientist as Sir J. H. Jeans (*The Backgrounds of Science*) to conclude that perhaps in the last analysis the universe is nothing but mind. The repercussions of these recent understandings upon the traditional ideas of the "natural" and the "supernatural" are as profound and far-reaching as upon the older ideas of "body" and "soul." These ideas, like those regarding the human person, arose out of a dualism that seems no longer to correspond to known facts. God now seems to be not only present in the processes of nature, but creatively at work in and through them. We need a new formula that will express the concept of the creative presence of God in every dimension of reality and not merely in those aspects of reality that are not yet understood.

Not only is personality to be thought of in the wholeness of its interacting elements, but as a *process* in which continuity and change are indissolubly united. The living person is not only the result of growth; he *is* growth, a *becoming*, like reality itself of which he is a part. It is this capacity for continuous growth at the level of intelligence, emotional maturity, and the enrichment of values that gives a fourth dimension to human personality, differentiating it from all other orders of organic life. It is the fact of growth as process that makes it possible to give direction to the development of personality with reference to ends, either socially or self-chosen. Continuity renders growth cumulative and stable, while change provides the opportunity for the introduction of new factors influencing the character of growth.

Furthermore, personality is dynamic, not passive. On the lower levels, the irrational impulses of original nature are ceaselessly reaching out toward those objects and activities that are capable of giving satisfaction. On the higher rational levels these outreachings are transmuted into desires. On the highest level these desires are sorted, evaluated, and organized into a system of values and subjected to the discipline of the desire to have certain kinds of desires. It is in

the consciousness of these desires as desires, in the discrimination of them, and in the deliberate pursuit of them in
action that the good life consists.

It is amazing that education has been so slow in recognizing the active nature of the growing person and in adap-
ting its content and method to it. The traditional techniques
of education thought of as instruction or training were based
upon a passive conception of pupils. To Johann F. Herbart
the mind was a blank tablet upon which knowledge was to
be inscribed by teachers through use of the famous "five
formal steps." To those who, with John Locke, held the
disciplinary view, education consisted of the imposition of
adult-chosen behavior patterns upon the plastic pupil
through habit formation or the conditioning of reflexes.
This is the method used for training animals. Not until
near 1900, and especially during the second quarter of this
century, has it become clear to teachers that they are dealing
with dynamic and forthreaching persons for whom learning
should be not an imposed task, but an exciting and rewarding
achievement. Under the influence of this insight, with most
good teachers the center of education is shifting from *teaching* to *learning* under the understanding and inspiring guidance of wise counselors.

II

Many factors affect the development of personality. At
the base of all the others are the bodily structures of the
human organism. These are biologically inherited and follow the combination of genes in the immediate and remote
ancestral line. A hereditary abnormality may doom the new-
born to idiocy, imbecility, or the limited mental and moral
capacity of the moron. Accident or disease may damage or
destroy nerve or brain tissue necessary to normal living and
moral responsibility. The formula, "A sane mind in a sound
body," while it may smack of dualistic implications, nevertheless records the sound judgment that, other things being

equal, abounding mental, moral, and spiritual health is dependent upon a sound and healthy physical organism. This
is why medical and dental care and physical education are
of primary importance in the school program. In many
cases the first step in remedial treatment of abnormal or
maladjusted children and young people should be a trip to
the clinic.

Only a slight step above the physical structures are the
reflexes. These are inherited predispositions of the organism
to respond to more or less specific stimuli or situations in
the environment in more or less predetermined patterns.
They are part of the equipment of original nature and as
such are unlearned. They are automatic, not conscious or
reasoned, as in the case of the dilation of the pupil of the eye
in response to light, the secretion of the adrenal glands in
the presence of danger or combat, or the withdrawal of the
hand from a hot object. This, together with instinct, is the
predominant level upon which animals live, and their behavior is modified by the technique of the conditioned
reflex. Amazingly enough, there is a philosophy and technique of education for humans based upon this method of
controlling animal behavior. This is not to suggest that the
training of the reflexes has no place in the education of
human beings. Far from it. But to base human education
upon this level of behavior is to falsify human nature and to
neglect its most significant capacities. After all, as C. Judson
Herrick (*Brains of Rats and Men*) has pointed out, human
beings are men, not rats. Nevertheless, a program of moral
and spiritual values in education would be blind or foolhardy
to ignore or underestimate the immense importance of the
automatic reflex in influencing human behavior.

Closely related to the automatic reflexes in their influence
upon the development of personality are the irrational impulses. These also are inborn tendencies to respond to more
or less definite situations in more or less definite and char-

acteristic patterns, though somewhat less precise and fixed
than in the case of reflexes. In the days of William James
these were known as "instincts," but by the time of E. L.
Thorndike they were coming to be thought of as irrational
impulses. They are rooted in the basic universal drives of the
organism for the satisfaction of organic needs, such as hunger,
sex, defense. At their higher levels they assume the form of
fundamental "wishes"—for recognition, intimacy, security,
and new experience. These furnish the rich subsoil in which
are rooted desires and values. The development of the wholesome personality must take full account of these primitive,
inborn outreachings of the self toward satisfying objects and
relations in the natural, social, and cosmic world. Happiness
and self-fulfillment largely depend upon the constructive
organization, discipline, and satisfaction of these drives; their
denial or repression leads to frustration and compensatory
or escape mechanisms of behavior.

Recent psychological studies have brought to teachers a
new appreciation of a hitherto little-understood factor in the
development of personality—the unconscious. The human
being's conscious, intellectual, and rationally purposeful behavior constitutes a relatively shallow overlay above a deep
and dark pool of the subconscious mechanisms of behavior.
In these dark recesses are stored the "forgotten" memories
of past experience. The psychoanalyist and the psychiatrist
have discovered that typical modes of abnormal behavior
otherwise inexplicable are directly traceable to conditions of
past experience so deeply repressed or so long forgotten that
the person himself is wholly unconscious of them and quite
unable by himself to recall them. They have devised subtle
techniques, such as dream interpretation, free association,
and the undirected interview, for exploring these dark cav-
erns of the mind and for helping the distressed person to
recover and face these suppressed memories. This is why
modern schools are developing programs of personal coun-

Moral and Spiritual Values

seling, with a psychiatrist on the staff or otherwise available.

Under the influence of the social sciences, and particularly of social psychology, a new and great importance has come to attach to social interaction as a factor in the development of personality. As G. H. Mead has pointed out (*Mind, Self, and Society*), increasingly it has become clear that the self is a social product. Even the consciousness of self is the result of a two-dimensional interaction with the objective world—the I-it sense arising from the interaction of the emerging self with the objects of nature and the I-thou sense growing out of the interaction of the growing self with other selves. At the same time there has occurred an understanding of the powerful influence of the role which the person assumes or is assigned in the various social groups of which he is a member. Since these roles are different and often in conflict in different groups, one of the most important and difficult responsibilities of those who guide the growth process of self-realizing persons is to help them achieve a supreme self-chosen role which makes it possible for them to evaluate these varying roles and to reconcile their conflicts. In his study of delinquency in Chicago, Clifford Shaw (*Delinquency Areas*) found that the influence of social environment is so great that it is possible to determine statistically the probability of a child's becoming a delinquent according to his residence in the zones surrounding the Loop in Chicago.

As we ascend the hierarchy of factors that influence the development of personality from the animal to the distinctively human level we encounter intelligence. By his capacity for understanding it is possible for the growing human being to become conscious of himself as a person and of his many-sided relations to the natural, social, and cosmic world. It becomes possible for him to analyze the situations to which he responds for their factors and possible outcomes, to search the accumulated records of past experience in the sciences, humanities, and the arts for knowledge and values by which to interpret the situations and to weigh the possible outcomes, and to execute his decisions effectively. It is this capacity to think creatively that most decisively differentiates man from the lower animals. It is the basis of his culture and of his control, within limits, over his natural world and social relations. Out of his capacity to think has grown his science, philosophy, history, literature, and the arts and crafts. Through it he is able to react selectively to his environment and thus to give direction to his experience and bring it under a measure of control. It is at this level of critical intelligence that education, especially in its moral and spiritual phases, should move, without in any sense neglecting or underrating the other factors influencing the development of personality.

But it is at the highest level of human behavior that we come upon the factor of values. It is this capacity to sort one's experiences, to project near and distant goals, and to devise means for their achievement that lifts intelligent human behavior to its highest attainment. At this level the impulsive outreach of the dynamic person is transmuted into disciplined desire. It is through the discrimination of values and preferential choices among them that a judgment of what is good and what is evil is possible and a hierarchy of values in which the good is subordinated to the best can be built. Such discrimination and choice make possible an organized system of values and a working philosophy of life which is the indispensable basis for any significant sense of meaning and worth in the human adventure.

And what is of equal significance is that values not only set the ends of living and give direction to experience, but they furnish the motivation to action. Desire and value in human behavior are only different but inseparable aspects of an undifferentiated process that binds the human being and the object it seeks together in a total behavior pattern. What appears as desire in the person appears as value in the desired object. And since desires are the mainsprings of action, it is here that the motivation of the good life is to be sought. A fundamental weakness of external and authoritative programs of moral education lies in the fact that they leave unsolved a problem—how to get children and young people to do what we think they know they ought to do. Therefore their appeal to external incentives in the form of reward and punishment, whereas a program built upon actual experience in making choices in real life situations with reference to self-chosen ends carries its own intrinsic motivation.

Moreover, at this creative level intelligence and values are inseparable. The integrity of the thinking process is a moral quality, while at the same time the validity of the moral judgment has its foundation in intelligent discrimination of facts and values. Up to the limits of a given person's intelligence, good intention is not in itself an adequate criterion or support of the good life. The first step in a moral act is being as intelligent about it as it is possible to be.

III

It is clear, therefore, that a program of moral and spiritual values in education is concerned with orders of personality. At the lowest end of the scale is a wholly disorganized personality—pathological at worst, or arrested and unorganized at best. Between multiple impulses or desires and inconsistent ideas, the self, inundated by an onrush of unassimilated raw experiences, is confused and torn by inner conflict and frustration. At the opposite end of the scale are well-organized, stable, and wholesome personalities whose behavior in a given set of circumstances can be predicted fairly definitely. It should be the primary concern of all education, but especially that which emphasizes moral and spiritual values, to assist growing persons to achieve an integrated, stable, and constantly developing personality. To this supreme end knowledge and techniques should be relevant and subordinate means.

Such a wholesome order of personality is an *achievement* of a self-realizing person, directed toward self-chosen ends and controlled by informed intelligence, and not merely the *result* of chance or externally imposed circumstances. The task of moral and spiritual education is to help self-realizing persons to discover the potential values as they emerge from their experience in the course of everyday living and to test them by the insights and values of the human past, interpret them, and judge them so as to bring their experience under the discipline of a controlling purpose.

The implication of these considerations is quite obviously that personality is the outgrowth of experience. The task of education is to help the growing person to understand his experience and to bring it under the control of ideas and values.

CHAPTER FIVE

The Nature of Experience
and Its Control

IF GIVEN the original nature with which the human being is born, personality is the result of the experiences which persons have, it logically follows that the way to control the development of personality is through control of the growing person's experience. Such control will be possible through an understanding of the source of experience, of its structure, and of the factors that determine outcomes of given units of experience. If the fullest possible development of desirable personality by self-realizing persons is the objective of education, and of moral and spiritual education in particular, the procedures by which experience is given quality and direction constitute method.

I

The source from which all experience derives is the interaction of the person with his objective world. Experience is thus bipolar—a sensitive, responding, and forthreaching organism on the one hand, and a stimulating, dynamic, and expanding environment on the other.

At birth the organism is comprised of the structures and capacities transmitted by heredity in an organization known as original nature. As soon, however, as its interaction with its environment begins—which is immediately—modifications occur, so that what at birth was original nature is on the way to becoming human nature. This is why in a growing person it is extremely difficult, if not impossible, to determine at any given stage of development what is due to original nature and what is due to interaction with the environment.

This difficulty is the ground for the old controversy regarding the relative influence of heredity and environment in the development of personality. On the whole, the psy-

THE SOURCE OF EXPERIENCE

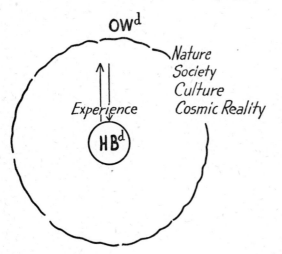

Fig. 1 The process of interaction between the human being and his objective world from which experience arises. HB, human being. OW, objective world consisting of nature, society, culture, and the cosmic reality. Coefficient d indicates the dynamic nature of both the human being and the objective world. Arrows indicate the reciprocal interaction of HB and OW.

chologists have tended to emphasize heredity, while the sociologists incline to stress environment. But the truth seems to lie with neither heredity nor environment conceived as independent and isolated factors. Rather it seems to rest upon the *functional union* of both in the interaction of the organism and the environment, as a result of which both are modified. Neither the human organism nor the objec-

tive world is static. Both are highly dynamic. Both are
processes in which continuity and change are indissolubly
united.[1] As a result of the interaction of the human person
and environment in contact, neither is imposed upon the
other. Through their functional union in the life process,
neither remains the same; neither is the result of the mere
addition of elements of the one to elements of the other. Out
of the interaction of the two something new, and in many
instances creative, emerges. And that something new is a
changed person on the one hand, and a changed environment
on the other. Together, in their largest collective dimensions,
these constitute a people's culture.

So much for the growing person. On the other hand, the
objective world is complex, dynamic, and vastly extended.
It consists in part of nature, in part of society, in part of the
accumulated traditions of culture, and in part of the vast
extensions of cosmic reality.

To the child the natural world presents itself as the physical objects and processes of his immediate environment.
Its intricate and manifold variety of form and color affords
him endless delight and satisfies his physical needs for survival and well-being. It was Friedrich Froebel's belief that
there is a mystical character in nature that evokes a spiritual
response from the child. Toyohiko Kagawa has criticized
religious education in America on the ground that it makes
so little of nature in the cultivation of spiritual attitudes.
As a youth, the growing person is brought into practical
working relation with the forces of nature and learns to appreciate and rely upon its orderliness and dependability.
As a student of the sciences he acquires an insight into the
vastness of the stellar universe and into the infinite complexity of the microcosmic world, as well as into the structure
of the elements and, most recently, of the atom. As a result

---

[1] For the concept of process in the objective world, see A. N. Whitehead,
Process and Reality.

of this interaction with nature man has attained his scientific knowledge on the one hand, and nature has yielded within limits to man's purpose and control on the other.

Similarly, the child's social world is immediate and personal, consisting of parents and relatives and the intimate neighborhood. School introduces him to a wider complex of social relationships that require definition and fulfillment. With maturation, his social world comes to include the community, the state, the nation, race and culture, and, under contemporary conditions, One World suddenly brought into physical, intellectual, and emotional contact, with its conflicting ideologies, cultural orientations, national loyalties, and organizations of power. If, as Mead has pointed out, the self is a social product, and, as Henry Churchill King once suggested, the richness and quality of one's life consists of the number of relations one discerns and fulfills, the interaction of the growing person with his social world is a most fertile source of moral and spiritual values.

It is out of man's historic interactions with his natural, social, and cosmic world that his accumulated traditions have grown through many millenia. These in their interrelatedness constitute his culture. They comprehend his science, his philosophy, his technology, his institutions, his religion, and his arts. For this reason our generation does not face its objective world *de novo*. This cultural heritage contains the resources of growing knowledge by which to interpret our present experience, of growing values by which to judge it, and of techniques by which to control it. So impressive and valuable is this cultural heritage that it is little wonder that traditional education has conceived its function to be the recovery and transmission of this precious heritage through instruction. More recently we are coming to see that the business of education is not, as Columbia University's President Nicholas Murray Butler, a good Herbartian, once affirmed (*The Meaning of Education*), to adjust the young to the traditions of culture, but to assist the young to achieve a creative interaction with their world with the help of man's past experience as preserved to us in the great traditions.

And beyond the immediately observable world of nature, society, and culture stretches the vast cosmic world, both spatially and temporally beyond the limits of imagination. Deeper and deeper penetrations into its mysterious unknown indicate that the cosmic world is continuous with our known world rather than an entirely different order of existence. This cosmic world is, as far as we know, the whole of reality. However one may interpret this world philosophically or theologically, it is the locus of those creative forces that have brought the universe into being and that sustain it within a vast comprehending framework of a rational and moral structure. Before that Reality the sensitive human spirit stands in awe and reverence, with a heightened sense of the meaning of human destiny and moral obligation. The interaction of the growing person with his objective world cannot be said to be complete until the increasingly mature and sensitive whole self responds to the whole of reality, both known and unknown, of which he is a part.

Even when the capacities of the dynamic human self and the complexity of the dynamic environment are so sketchily outlined, it is clear that the experience which grows out of their interaction is fraught not only with intellectual insights, but with moral and spiritual values. The problem of moral and spiritual education is to develop sensitivity to these values, to discover them, and to cultivate them.

II

Such being the source of experience, the next problem in moral and spiritual education is how to bring experience under self-control and give it direction toward self-chosen ends. Obviously the approach to this problem is through an understanding of the structure of experience and the factors of change that operate in and through that structure.

Now, when any given unit of experience is subjected to analysis, it reveals a definite structure. That structure consists of three elements: (1) an identifiable situation, (2) an identifiable response, and (3) the psychological processes that unite the situation and the response.

A UNIT OF EXPERIENCE

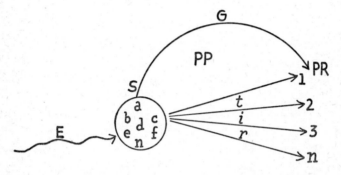

Fig. 2 The structure of a unit of experience. E, experience under way. S a-n, an identifiable situation and the complex of factors involved. G, the gap that occurs between the situation and the response. PR 1-n, the possible identifiable responses that may be made to the situation. PP t-r, the thinking, impulsive, or reflexive psychological process by which the response is united with the situation in a completed act.

The situation presents itself as some aspect of the environing world, capable of evoking a response from the sensitive human organism. It may be, and often is, a simple situation with a single predominant stimulus, as when the hand is withdrawn from a sharp object causing pain. Or it may be, and at the human level most often is, complex, involving many factors. The more informed and sensitive the growing person becomes through experience and education, the more

aware he is of the complexity of any given situation, of many
of the apparently simple ones, and of their interrelation with
other situations. Professor Basil L. Gildersleeve once re-
marked that if one started with the apparently most trivial
and commonplace event and explored its implications fully,
such exploration would take one to the limits of the universe.
Such complex situations are involved in the choice of a
vocation, in the decision of what is right and what is wrong
in the conflict of roles in differing social groups, and in
making up one's mind about a constructive course of action
in the present world crisis between totalitarian Russia and
the free nations. This is why in actual conduct virtues are
never abstractions and can never really be determined apart
from the specific circumstances of the concrete behavior
situation. One of the most persistent sources of error in
moral judgments is to oversimplify the situation. One's
correct "reading" of the multiple factors in any given situation is the first step in a moral decision regarding it, and
this is an act of discriminating, selective intelligence. If
through lack of knowledge or inattention one responds to
an inconsequential factor rather than to the essential one in
a behavior situation, the resulting conduct will be wrong at
worst or irrelevant at best.

The Gestaltists have emphasized not only the complexity of
behavior situations, but the interrelatedness of their factors.
They point out that one's response is to the total configuration of the situation and not to an isolated stimulus or to a
group of separate stimuli. The response is to a luminous
point on a broad background of interrelated stimuli. Thus,
the simple response of taking an umbrella or raincoat when
going out in threatening weather is a response to what, upon
reflection, is a fairly complex configuration of stimuli—the
forecast of the weather bureau, the appearance of the sky,
the feel of the atmosphere, the sight of other pedestrians

carrying umbrellas or raincoats, the memory of a cold contracted under similar conditions, and the possibility of being drenched.

The identifiable response as the second element in the structure of a given unit of experience also may be simple and immediate or complex and delayed. Innumerable everyday behaviors are of this simple and immediate character, such as shaving, eating one's breakfast, stepping up at the curb, or bidding a neighbor good morning. Many of them have been reduced to habit, so that the response is automatic, instantaneous, and for the most part unconscious. On the other hand, behaviors involving crucial decisions are complicated by many possibilities, the examination of many factors, and sustained deliberation. The choice of and preparation for a vocation, the choice of a life companion, voting on an involved political issue—these are only suggestions of those major situations upon the outcome of which may depend the entire course of one's life, even though they may occur but once.

The third element in the structure of experience is the psychological process that intervenes between the situation and the response and that binds situation and response together in a completed act. This integrating bond may take place on three levels—the reflexive or automatic, the irrational-impulsive, or the reflective-purposive.

On the automatic level the reflexes determine the immediate and quite uniformly characteristic responses, inherited, unlearned, and present at birth. Such automatic responses are also made on the basis of habit, even though the original responses occurred on either of the higher levels. Through habit, recurrent responses become "second nature." Thus habit, while it may stereotype undesirable behavior patterns and render them inflexible, may, if deliberately adopted and subject to change, render a great service of economy by relieving the person of having to go through the process of deliberation and choice in every recurrent situation, as in the case of paying bills promptly or of observing the standardized amenities of social intercourse.

More than most of us would like to admit, our responses to life situations take place on the irrational, impulsive level. The fundamental impulses, or "wishes," are much older, much deeper, and much better organized than our intelligence. As a consequence, the growing person finds himself acting in response to his imperious desires and afterwards attempting to justify his action on rational grounds. This is known as "rationalization" as distinguished from reflective thinking in advance of the consummation of the act.

The highest response to life situations takes place on the reflective-purposive level. On this level experience reaches its most characteristically human quality. The situation is analyzed for its essential factors on the one hand, and the response for its possibilities on the other. A deliberate and systematic search is made of one's own past experience and of the accumulated experience of the race for the knowledge that will enable one to understand the experience, for values and standards by which to judge the alternative possible outcomes, and for techniques for managing the situation. On the basis of such an analysis and appraisal one among the possible outcomes is chosen and carried through to a completed act. If the outcome chosen proves not to be satisfactory or the means used is not successful, a new and better analysis of the situation is attempted or a different method is employed.[1] At this highest level one's attitudes and behavior are brought under the control of informed intelligence and an organized set of values. As reflective-purposive behavior it is definitely oriented toward the achievement of self-chosen ends and is directed toward these ends by reflec-

[1] For an analysis of the complete act of thought, see John Dewey, *How We Think*.

tive thinking. Experience has become creative and at the same time and by the same process morally responsible and spiritually sensitive.

The process by which conduct is determined through the selective use of factors in a situation and choice among possible outcomes as set forth in Fig. 2, may be illustrated by the incident of cheating by some ninety cadets in the United States Military Academy, currently widely publicized and discussed in the press.

Upon analyzing the situation, which in this case is quite complex, a number of crucial factors appear. (1) The Academy is the training institution for the nation's army officers who will be trusted with the fortunes of war and the lives of countless young men in battle. As such it has the tradition of unqualified integrity and honor. (2) To embody and maintain this ideal it has an honor system enforced by rigorous discipline. (3) It also has a football team with a tradition of winning. (4) Football practice and games make an extremely heavy demand upon the time and energy of the players. (5) In order to remain in the Academy and achieve a record upon which future professional status in the army may depend, the players must get good grades. (6) The system of examinations is such that identical examinations are given to different groups at different times, thus making cheating relatively easy. (7) The prestige of the Academy would be gravely damaged if it were found out that cheating occurred. (8) It is said that some cadets have cheated in the past and gotten away with it.

On the other hand, there are several possible outcomes among which the cadet may choose. (1) At great effort he might prepare for the examination under unfavorable conditions and do the best he can, even at the cost of lower grades. (2) He might give up his place on the football squad and devote all his time and energies to study. (3) He might resign from the Academy and seek a football career in a

civilian institution in which the honor system is not in vogue.
(4) He might take a calculated or blind risk of cheating
in the hope that his cheating would not be discovered.

As for the level on which he makes his choice there are
several alternatives. (1) He might act on the wholehearted
personal acceptance of unswerving honesty, no matter at
what cost. (2) He might think through the consequence of
a dishonorable act of cheating upon the lofty standards of
his profession, the effect which such an act would have upon
the prestige of the Academy, and its influence upon his own
character. (3) He might yield to his fear of failure and to
what, under pressure, appears to be his immediate self-
interest. (4) He might uncritically feel that after all cheating
on an examination is not a serious misdemeanor, especially
since it is understood that it is often practiced in higher institutions of learning and has occurred in the Academy.

In this case some ninety cadets reacted to factors (4), (5),
and (6) in the situation. Of the possible outcomes they
chose (4). As for levels of response, they acted on (3) and
(4).

The result, as we all know, was tragic, ending with dismissal from the Academy, a severe compromise of their
professional future, and a humiliating national scandal. Perhaps no incident could better illustrate the place of moral
and spiritual values in meeting and responding to a practical
conduct situation.

III

How then is experience to be controlled? The answer lies
in the foregoing analysis of the structure of experience and
of the factors by which concrete and specific responses are
made to concrete and specific life situations which the human
being encounters in his interaction with his objective world.
It is by consciously and intentionally selecting or modifying
the factors that determine the way in which responses are
made to situations. What is done to modify these factors

depends upon the level on which the response is made, whether it be automatic, impulsive, or reflective-purposive. Since the behavior of the person includes responses on all three levels, none of these factors should be neglected, but all should be dealt with in any constructive program of moral and spiritual education.

When educators face the responsibility of controlling the experience of children and young people a major issue immediately presents itself: what kind of control shall there be and who shall exercise it, and what relative emphasis shall be placed upon the respective factors. If children and young people are thought of as passive subjects to be molded by adults into predetermined modes of thought and action, then education will be external and authoritative. The primary emphasis will be placed upon the reflexes and the impulses, and the method will take the form of the conditioned reflex, habit formation, and the organization of the irrational emotions. If, on the other hand, children and young people are thought of as active and responsible persons, the control sought will be self-control, education will be creative, and the primary emphasis will be upon reflective thinking and purposive action, always, of course, on the level of maturing capacities and under understanding adult guidance. Education in a totalitarian state, whether Hitlerian or Soviet, follows the first type and is a process of ruthless regimentation. Education in a democracy, on the contrary, places the supreme emphasis upon the self-realization of the individual, upon the ability to think factually and critically, and upon co-operation toward commonly chosen ends by the use of commonly chosen means. The aim of the teacher is to help growing persons to condition their own reflexes, to discipline their own emotions, to choose their own ends, and to use their own intelligence in attaining them.

Manifestly, in this latter type of education through creative experience, values play an indispensable part. They pro-

CHAPTER SIX

The Functional Relation of Values to Experience

IF VALUES are of such fundamental importance in the education of self-realizing persons, where are those who are responsible for the education of children and young people to look for them? Upon the answer to this question will depend the method employed for their discovery and development. It is with regard to this issue that the basic differences in the approach to so-called character education arise. If moral and spiritual values have their origin outside human experience and have to be imported into it from some supposed "supernatural" order, the method obviously will be external and authoritative and will assume the form of inculcation. The same will be true if these values reside in the adult members of society and have to be transferred to its immature members. If, on the other hand, moral and spiritual values inhere in the nature of human experience and grow out of it, the procedure will be of a fundamentally different order. It will take the form of helping growing persons to become aware of their experience, to become sensitive to these values as they emerge from the relations and functions of everyday living, and to bring them to their full functioning in the motivation and control of that experience.

I

In any case, if moral and spiritual values are to be real and vital in the lives of children and young people they must be *experienced*. That is why presenting them as abstractions and verbalizing *about* them are bafflingly ineffective, with little or no measurable influence upon conduct.

Herein lies the fundamental criticism of the "trait" approach to character education. To begin with, the traits are abstractions, such as honesty, truthfulness, loyalty, obedience, humility. More than that, they are sought for in adult experience, either by the analysis of adult activity or by a consensus of adult opinion. These traits are then listed for systematic "teaching" by the standard Herbartian method of instruction. Once they have been "learned," the final step consists of looking about for the life situations in which they may be "applied." This done, the teacher or parent then faces the leftover problem of getting the child or youth to want to do what presumably he knows he ought to do, but which he has no incentive for doing.[1]

As a matter of fact, this approach exactly reverses the normal process by which persons of all ages learn in actual life situations. Traits are the generalized outcomes of past experience in many concrete situations and over long periods of time. Normal learning begins in experience and ends in experience. Ways of acting are the outcomes of dealing with concrete and specific situations, as outlined in Chapter V. They can never, except in the most general way, be predicted in advance of the specific circumstances. Thus, what is loyalty in one set of circumstances may be quite different from loyalty in another set of circumstances. Instead of looking around for situations in which to "apply" an abstract and generalized trait, learning should begin with the situation and work itself through by analysis of the situation and its possible outcomes, the utilization of the end products of past racial experience, choice among alternatives, and decision to the completed act. Only by some such creative

1 For a detailed outline of this procedure, see W. W. Charters, *The Teaching of Ideals*.

procedure can that most difficult of all lines in education be crossed—the line between verbalization and action. And only so can those incentives that are inherent in the purposive act be counted on to carry through.

This is true because values, like ideas, sustain a functional relation to experience. On the one hand, they grow out of experience; on the other, they re-enter it as factors of control in determining the ends of purposive action, in providing criteria for judgments, and in supplying motivation.

It should be noted, however, that the validity or fundamental importance of the identification and clear apprehension of traits of character is not here questioned. The issue involved is whether these traits or virtues are inherent in experience or are extraneous to experience and have to be imported into it. The issue also concerns the place at which character traits or virtues appear in the process of normal experience; that is, whether they come before experience or as experience nears consummation in the completed act. Any program of moral and spiritual education that fails definitely to identify these traits of good character and to erect them into norms of desirable behavior and into ideals to be striven for is hopelessly defective. This was the merit of the McGuffey readers of a past generation. They made the virtues of honesty, truthfulness, loyalty, fidelity, and kindness vivid as the enduring achievements of a humane and civilized life and as the expectations of the Great Society, so that they could be shared and taken over like the "mother tongue." In the procedure here expounded these virtues are in no sense overlooked or neglected. The difference is that they are used primarily as resources of racial experience in helping children and young people achieve these ideals creatively. In any case, whether they come first in a program of inculcation or as the crowning achievement of a creative experience of learning, they are the indispensable foundations of the good life.

In this connection another consideration arises about the
capacity of children and young people to enter into the
process of reflective and critical thinking involved in a
genuinely creative experience, as outlined in Chapter V.
Manifestly, normal or superior intelligence is necessary for
the higher forms of critical analysis and discriminating choice,
and it would be expecting the impossible to suppose that
all children and young people can rise to this level of
creative experience. For those in the lower ranges of intelligence dependence should be placd upon participation in
the social group where moral and spiritual values are being
discovered and developed and, in some cases, upon verbal
precept and habit formation. Even so, it will be found that
active participation in a group where these values are coming
into being and are functioning in the control of conduct
will be found more vital and effective than verbal precept or
the direct method of habit formation. Nevertheless, every
effort should be made by teachers to insure the fullest possible content of thinking and discriminating choice in the
discovery and development of moral and spiritual values.

II

Interestingly enough, the psychological situation in which
values arise is the same as that in which reflective thinking
arises. Not only do they both belong to the highest order of
human capacity and activity, but they are inseparably related
in the forthreaching of the human organism toward desired
ends.

All values rest ultimately upon the inborn capacities and
impulses to lay hold upon those objects in the environment
that are capable of bringing satisfaction—organic hungers for
food, sex, rhythm, and comfort, and the so-called "wishes"
for recognition, intimacy, security, and new experience. At
the subhuman animal level these impulses pass directly
through predetermined mechanisms of reflex and instinct

from yearning to satisfaction, without being raised into consciousness. Much of human behavior is on this instinctive level. As long as the action is uninterrupted and free-flowing, neither the end nor the act is raised into vivid consciousness. Impulse passes directly through the appropriate action to satisfaction.

In the more characteristically human behavior, however, a gap occurs between the impulse and its fulfillment. This delayed response is caused by the interruption of the forth-reaching action that unites the longing self with the longed-for object. It may be caused by some form of blockage or by the necessity of choosing between two or more possible alternatives.

The first result of the delayed response is to raise the object sharply into consciousness and at the same time the wish to obtain it. The second result is to transform what before was an unconscious or dimly recognized wish into conscious desire. Desire on the part of the self clothes the desired object with value because of its capacity to satisfy the desire. Thus the valuing experience is bipolar: in the subject it appears as desire; in the object it appears as value. There can be no desire for an object that is incapable of bringing satisfaction; no object can possess value that does not evoke desire.

The gap caused by the interruption or blockage of action between the desiring subject and the valued object is filled up with delay, suspense, and effort. Anything that causes delay between desire and its fulfillment tends to intensify desire and at the same time to heighten the sense of value attaching to the thing desired, except that the delay must not be too long. In that event, the hope of attaining the object may be abandoned, and the seeking self may surrender to frustration, indifference, or despair. As an ancient Hebrew proverb has it, "Hope deferred maketh the heart sick; but when the desire cometh, it is a tree of life."

In the same way uncertainty and suspense intensify desire and heighten the sense of value. As long as attainment is certain, even in the face of considerable delay, desire may remain casual. But when attainment of the end desired passes under the shadow of uncertainty, both desire and the sense of value are accentuated in something like direct ratio to the degree of suspense. A person in excellent health and vigor is scarcely conscious of health except as a sense of general well-being. But if some vital organ, like the heart, ceases to function properly, one becomes vividly conscious of the value of health and will go to any length to recover it. Things that are quite secure tend to be taken for granted; but let them be placed in jeopardy, and at once they become highly appreciated. Thus in America we had come to take our freedom for granted. But now that our liberties and those of the free world are placed in extreme peril by the aggression of Soviet Russia, we have quite suddenly become aware of the priceless value of freedom and are setting about to defend it at incredible expenditure of means and life.

Effort has the same effect in enhancing desire and value as have delay and suspense. That which one acquires with little or no effort or cost tends to be esteemed lightly. Thus a young man born into an affluent family with a tradition that as a matter of course all children will attend college may take quite casually his going to college, whereas the young person born into a family of meager resources where going to college entails great sacrifices and earning one's own way is almost certain to take his college education seriously as a precious opportunity.

Significantly, as regards motivation in learning, especially perhaps in the realm of moral and spiritual values, the reverse is also true. A valued, and therefore desired, end is capable of evoking sustained effort necessary for its attainment. This is true because there is a transfer of value from the end sought to the means for its attainment. When learning is concerned with ends that are felt by the learner to be of value to him, directly or indirectly, the learning process, as John Dewey pointed out (*Interest and Effort*), carries its own inherent motivation, and eliminates the necessity of appealing to extrinsic incentives, such as rewards and punishment. It is one of the anomalies of educational philosophy

How Values Arise

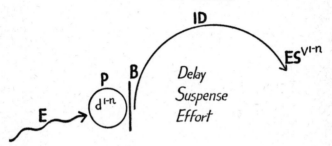

Fig. 3 The psychological situation in which values arise. E, experience under way. P, the person. B, blockage of experience. ES, end sought. ID, interval of delay between desire and its realization. d^{1-n}, desire heightened by degree of delay, suspense, or effort. v^{1-n}, value attached to end sought correspondingly heightened by degree of delay, suspense, or effort.

that the transfer of value from the end product of learning to the effort involved was so complete in the disciplinary theory of education that the effort involved in learning came to be more esteemed than the thing learned.

It should be added that in this gap created by the delayed response, emotions are generated, among them some of the most profound known to human experience, as well as reflective thinking and values. Consequently, when thinking is concerned with the practical issue of living it is not normally a cold intellectual process, but warm with feeling. For this reason, however, care should be taken that the emotions do not destroy the objectivity of thinking.

For the purposes of this volume it has not seemed necessary or advisable to enter upon a discussion of the various metaphysical theories of value. It has seemed sufficient to deal with the psychological processes by which values emerge from experience and function in the appraisal, direction, and motivation of experience. It may be said, however, that the process of the interaction of the human being with his natural, social, and cosmic world as interpreted in this discussion assumes the objective existence of a world of reality that is progressively discovered through experience of it. As science has disclosed a structure of intelligible and orderly processes in nature, so man's agelong experience seems indubitably to disclose a moral structure. This moral structure as it has progressively come to light through successive generations of mortal men transcends any historical period, though man's interpretation of it has changed as his experience has yielded deeper insights and wider perspectives, precisely as his conception of the nature of the physical world has changed with new scientific discoveries. Nor is this process of discovery by any means complete. In the light of man's cultural history it is to be expected that as man's understanding of the structure and behavior of the physical world has immensely increased in modern times, so his understanding of the moral order and behavior of reality will deepen and widen as he increasingly interacts with the complex details of reality, as is impressively suggested by the growing ethical insights and standards of historic cultures, including the great historic religious systems like Judaism and Christianity.

III

There is another way than this individualistic one in which values are derived from experience. It is through participation in the social group in which values are operative. Values, like personality itself, are social as well as personal. Through long experience, values derived from

personal experience are shared and absorbed into the collective attitudes, mores, morals, standards, and institutions
of society. These furnish the criteria by which a society
judges the conduct of its members. These values the individual takes over unconsciously because they are functionally
a part of the life process. In the area of moral and spiritual
attitudes these social values are extremely potent. They
have the sanction and prestige of social acceptance. As one
takes over unconsciously his "mother tongue," so he takes
over the group's amenities, its taste, its ideas of right and
wrong, its religious beliefs and practices. If one's ideas or
conduct deviate too widely from the socially accepted norm,
positive social pressure is brought to bear upon him to secure
conformity.

The bearing of these considerations upon moral and spiritual education is profound. In spite of any formal program
of moral and spiritual education which a given school may
adopt, the values which are actually operative in the corporate life of the school are decidedly the most effective influence upon the moral and spiritual attitudes of the pupils.
The first step, therefore, in any such program should be an
examination and appraisal by the school of its own system
of operative values.

But the matter is even more complicated than that. Often
the standards which the school sincerely endeavors to develop
in its pupils run counter to those that are operative in the
environing community. When such is the case, efforts of the
school are greatly handicapped, if not rendered impotent.
Since the work of the school is not done in a vacuum, this
means that the school has the responsibility to help the
community to examine and improve its values.

The studies of Hugh Hartshorne and Mark May (*Studies
in Deceit*) and of Hedley S. Dimock (*Adolescent Behavior*)
have shown that participation in the social group is far more
influential in shaping ideals and conduct than formal in-

struction—so much so that Dr. Hartshorne (*Character in Human Relations*) has proposed social participation as a basis for character education. When it is recalled that personality is a social product, it is clear why the conscious and intentional organization of group life in the school is of such great importance in a program of moral and spiritual education.

IV

Moreover, it is out of many different kinds of experience in many different areas and relationships that inconsistencies and conflicts in values arise. These inconsistencies and conflicts may lead, without proper guidance, to confusion and frustration. Under proper guidance in the use of the creative procedure outlined in Chapter V, these inconsistencies and conflicts normally lead to discrimination of values. As a result of such discrimination, certain values are judged to be negative and therefore to be avoided, while others judged to be good are subordinated to those judged to be supremely worthful. In this way a hierarchy of values emerges. And when this hierarchy of values is attained under the influence of reflective thinking, the crowning result is a philosophy of life. When translated into the life process, it is a way of life.

V

The highest level in the organization of values is the revaluation of all values into a total meaning and worth of life. No program of moral and spiritual education can be considered to have achieved its goal until in some measurable degree it has risen to this level.

Viewed on the larger cultural scene, man in his interaction with his objective world has developed many practical interests and activities—economic, social, political, intellectual, esthetic, and moral. Each of these modes of interest and activity has its own specialized set of values. Under the conditions of modern life, activities in these several areas tend to become increasingly specialized and as a consequence the several sets of values incline to become self-contained and isolated. As a result, modern man's personal experience and culture tend to fall apart and to lose their meaning and worth. The most imperative need of contemporary culture is for some effective synthesis that will give wholeness to the common life and to the personalities of those who participate in it. This is pre-eminently the need of a democratic society with its emphasis upon freedom, in competition with the extreme corporate unity of the totalitarian state. In a totalitarian state such unity as it has may be attained through force; in a democracy it can only be achieved from within through the integration of values.

When the more or less independent values operative in these separate areas of experience are brought together at the functional center of all experiences, are fused and heightened into a total meaning and worth of life, personal and social life are seen and felt in their wholeness and interrelatedness. A new quality is added to experience that could not come from the pursuit of any one specialized interest, such as science, wealth, art, or party loyalty. Life in its integrated wholeness takes on an inspiring and releasing sense of meaning and worth.

More than that, once this integration of values is to a measurable extent under way, it reacts upon each of these specialized areas of interest and activity as a factor of cross-criticism and reconstruction. Thus economic activity, motivated by profit, is brought under the criticism of scientific intelligence, social consequences, and ethical judgment. Scientific research is brought to answer not only to its own canons of exacting truthfulness and objectivity, but to society for its economic, political, and moral responsibility. And so for every other interest and activity. No self-contained and self-centered value can remain the same when viewed in the perspective of every other value, and especially of the total meaning and worth of life in its many dimensions of interest and need and in responsible relation to total reality.

To the extent that this revaluation is present in experience, experience assumes a religious quality. This is religion functionally conceived, as distinguished from a theological or an ecclesiastical conception. This functional revaluation

REVALUATION OF VALUES

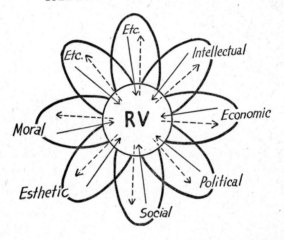

Fig. 4 The reciprocal relation of specialized values and the total meaning and worth of life resulting from the revaluation of all values. The outlying enclosures represent the different areas of experience and their specialized values: Intellectual (science, philosophy); Economic (production, consumption, exchange); Political (administration, policy, currency, judiciary); Social (personal and group relations, institutions); Esthetic (creating and enjoying beauty); Moral (moral behavior, ethics); Etc. (all other areas of experience). RV, the central area in which all specialized values are integrated and fused into a total meaning and worth of life. Solid arrows indicate the influence of specialized values upon the integrated core of values. Broken arrows indicate the critical and reconstructive influence of integrated values upon every specialized value.

of values, as the scientific study of religion has shown, is the basis of all the historic religions and of personal religious experience. Its theological concepts and ecclesiastical structures differ from one group to another and change from time to time as the interests and activities of the group change. The function of religion—the revaluation of all values—remains constant. It is an integral part of man's constitution, of his interaction with his objective world, and of his cultural heritage. It transcends all sectarian expressions and interpretations, and is to be identified with none of them.

The functional revaluing of values is an essential phase of the education of the whole person in relation to his whole world, and no program of education can be complete without this crowning achievement of the human spirit. Within the larger cultural pattern, with its highly developed specialized interests and activities and their respective systems of particular values into which he is born, the child faces the task of building his many and disparate experiences into a consistent and unified pattern of life. While his experiences are on a smaller personal scale, for him they are as significant as are the massive experiences of the adult world, and as difficult to understand and manage. As he matures he becomes increasingly involved in the major concerns of the adult world and feels the pull of their centrifugal force in a secular and fragmented culture. By so much the more is it essential to his personal integrity that he gradually achieve a revaluation of his own values and so discover for himself a sustaining, even a compelling, sense of the meaning and worth of his own life as a human person. In this he will need the understanding guidance of mature teachers who themselves have found the way to a meaningful life integrated around a set of values worthy of supreme devotion.

CHAPTER SEVEN

Values Are Indigenous
to the School Community

IN THE light of the nature and origin of experience and of the functional relation of values to it, the question is sharply raised about where teachers and administrators are to look for moral and spiritual values. The answer to this question will determine the basic pattern of procedure in any program of moral and spiritual education.

I

Analysis shows that most programs of character education in the school rest upon the implicit assumption that the school itself and the learning process are devoid of positive value content. Consequently, moral and spiritual values have to be imported from some external source and in many cases by agencies outside the school.

This is true of the various types of effort on the part of churches to introduce religious instruction into the schools, whether upon the initiative of the churches or school authorities. The predominant form of this approach is that of released time by which pupils are allowed time on the public school schedule to attend religious classes, upon the written request of parents. In most cases such instruction is given in church properties, in a lesser number of instances in public school buildings, a practice rendered illegal by the recent Supreme Court decision. In most cases the instruction is given by church teachers. In some instances it is given in periods outside the school schedule. The subject matter always is determined by the churches. Sometimes it is correlated with the school curriculum; sometimes it is not. Sometimes it is offered for school credit; sometimes no credit is received.

At the state university level the several faiths and denominations maintain chaplains and religious foundations adjacent to the campus for their student members. Sometimes religious courses are offered by the foundation, with or without credit by the university. The earliest form of this effort was that of Bible chairs established by a denomination near the university in which religious courses were offered, with or without credit. In other cases certain denominations and faiths have established co-operative schools of religion in connection with state universities.

In keeping with the principles outlined in Chapter III, it is not intended to raise the question of the validity of the theological or ecclesiastical interpretations of the source or nature of moral and spiritual values as held by the several faiths and denominations, or the bearing of these interpretations upon the problem here under consideration. The school should treat the religious beliefs and practices of individuals and religious groups with impartial respect and sympathetic understanding. Where questions of a theological or ecclesiastical nature arise in the school experience, the school will do well to refer the pupil to his parents or to his pastor.

The assumption of an absence of values in the school is the basis also, though less directly and more subtly, of most of the programs of so-called "character education" in the schools—notably so of the trait approach. These traits are not searched for in the experience of the school community, but in the adult experience by activity analysis or consensus of adult opinion. As a result, they confront the pupil as something external, foreign to his own experience, and authoritative. This necessitates the use of an external and authoritative method, designed, like the Herbartian with his subject matter and the blank mind of the learner, to impress these virtues upon passive, if not resistant, pupils.

All these approaches rest in a greater or less degree upon the assumption that moral and spiritual values are not intrinsically present, at least potentially, in the school community and the learning process, but have to be brought in from some outside source and imposed upon the school experience.

II

On the other hand, in the light of the nature of experience and of the functional relation of values to experience, as understood by the biological, psychological, and social sciences, moral and spiritual values are indigenous to the relations and functions of the school itself. More than that, if moral and spiritual values are to be real and vital and compelling in the life of the pupil they must grow out of these relations and function in them as intrinsic motivation and control.

It cannot be otherwise when the moral and spiritual are thought of, as they should be, as *qualities* of the responses which pupils make to actual life situations. A response is moral when it is made to a situation through a choice of possible outcomes in the light of the growing ethical insights of mankind through generations regarding what is good, and in the light of the personal and social demands of the situation itself. It is amoral when it is made without reference to these standards. It is immoral when it is made in violation of these standards.

Similarly, a response is spiritual when it is made in the widest perspectives of the world of reality and at the highest level of the capacities of the human spirit. In the light of the earlier discussion regarding the character of the natural world, the spiritual cannot be set off in radical contrast with the physical, neither can it be identified with the "super-

natural." It is awareness of and sensitivity to the creative
processes at work in nature, society, and the universe in the
realm of values, which in its totality has been associated by
mankind the world over with the concept of God. Moreover,
spirituality carries with it the idea of devotion to that which
is felt to be supremely worthful.

Thus, as John Dewey (*A Common Faith*) has pointed
out, at the level of experiencing (that is, the interaction of
the human being with his objective world) the moral and
the spiritual are always *qualities* of an experience (expressed
by the adjectives moral and spiritual), whereas the end
product of past experiences in its cumulative and system-
atized form is substantive (expressed by the nouns morality
and spirituality).

The problem of moral and spiritual education is, therefore, twofold. On the one hand, it is to help pupils to experience these values by making choices that are moral and
spiritual in their nature and carrying through their decisions
from intention to action in specific and concrete situations.
On the other hand, it is to help the pupils to build up their
many specific decisions and actions into generalized attitudes
toward all situations and into dependable patterns of behavior.

What teachers, supervisors, and administrators need to
realize is that whenever and wherever a response is being
made to a situation in the relations and activities of the
school, potential moral and spiritual values are involved.
What happens to these values depends entirely upon the
sensitivity and the awareness of teachers and pupils alike to
their presence and upon the skill with which teachers and
administrators help their pupils to make them actual, articulate, and effective.

Where, then, are we to look for these value potentials?
The answer is, in every specific relation and activity of the
school experience. One of the most fruitful areas will be the

relations and activities of the school as a community. It is
a fundamental error often made to think of the educative
process as being chiefly or wholly a matter of formal instruction involving subject matter, assignments, recitations,
examinations, and credit, and to think of the school community merely as a necessary administrative structure for
housing the educative process. In the long run, participation
in the school as a community probably has greater influence
upon the formation of the personality of the pupil than do
courses or the study of subject matter. This is particularly
true of the formation of social attitudes, the disposition and
ability to co-operate with others in common enterprises, the
formation of moral standards, and spiritual appreciations.
Like all communities, the school is a complex of relationships
—person-to-person, person-to-group, group-to-person, and
group-to-group. These relationships are mediated through
many activities, such as those involved in schedules, courses
of study, use of school property, home room, cafeteria, halls,
playground, sports, orchestra, and administration. They are
conditioned by many factors, such as group opinion, prejudice, custom, fads, "wishes." The fact that the pupil is en-
meshed in the intricate web of relations requiring discernment and fulfillment makes the school community a
particularly fertile field for the development of moral
judgments and spiritual appreciations. Out of these relations
arise behavior situations involving such moral judgments
and spiritual appreciations.

A second area of school experience in which moral and
spiritual values are inherent is the curriculum. In a particular way the school through its curriculum is the most
authentic interpreter of a people's culture. This is true
because the curriculum, especially that part which deals with
the heritage, contains the great traditions of man's cultural
achievement as preserved in the natural sciences, the humanities, the social sciences, and the arts. That part which deals

with life adjustment problems deeply involves the attitudes of contemporary society toward the issues regarding vocational choice in relation to personal development and the service that one may render to society. Every branch of the curriculum is rich in value potentials. The study of science is charged with such values as open-mindedness, the attitude of inquiry, respect for facts, disciplined intelligence, an understanding of the ordered structure of the universe, an appreciation of the vastness and mystery of a universe of unimaginable space and time dimensions. History can give a sense of process, of living on the growing edge of the human adventure, of the rooting of the present in the past, of the emergent future, of the ideas and values for which mankind has struggled, and of great historic persons who have embodied these ideas and values. The social studies offer an understanding and appreciation of society, the supreme worth of persons, the evolution of institutions and their relations to man's need, democracy as a society of free persons, tolerance and co-operation, and of differences as assets of social living. Literature and the arts present an interpretation and criticism of life in its wholeness, and the capacity to enter into the "great conversation" between generations through symbols—literature, painting, music, the plastic arts, architecture, and the drama. These moral and spiritual value potentials are indigenous in the curriculum and wait only to be discovered and made articulate.

A third area of school experience rich in moral and spiritual values is personal and group counseling. Since the development of personality depends so much upon the discernment and fulfillment of one's relations to nature and society, failures in making right adjustments are fraught with grave consequences. The school, therefore, has no greater educational opportunity or responsibility than to provide guidance to pupils in making normal adjustments and to give understanding counsel where maladjustments have occurred.

In this area teachers and pupils are concerned not only with understanding, but basically with values. The noted psychoanalist, C. G. Jung, has stated that the solutions for the problems in all his cases of persons more than thirty-five years old have involved essentially religious values (*Modern Man in Search of a Soul,* pp. 231, 235, 236, 245, 254). Here, as perhaps nowhere else, the teacher may help the pupil to build a value system and a philosophy of life.

A fourth direction in which to look for moral and spiritual values in the school experience is in the field of physical education, sports, and recreation. Besides being in many ways the most vivid of school experiences, these offer in an unusual way situations involving such qualities as personal and group integrity, loyalty, co-operation, courtesy, respect for the body, fairness, and that galaxy of traits known as sportsmanship. If coaches are sensitive to these values and seek the development of their charges rather than primarily the winning of contests, they have an unusual opportunity to develop these values and at the same time bear an unusual responsibility.

In a fifth area the school has unlimited opportunity to discover moral and spiritual values as they emerge in the school experience and to render them reproducible and communicable through symbols, ceremonies, and celebrations.

These are major areas, to be explored in some detail in Part III of this book, in which moral and spiritual values indigenous to the school community and the learning process are to be found. The sensitive teacher will find innumerable other situations in the course of school and classroom experience which yield rich veins of moral and spiritual values.

III

These considerations set the pattern of procedure for a program of moral and spiritual education in the school.

Such a procedure consists of four major phases which normally, though not always, have this sequence: (1) discovery, (2) identification, (3) development, and (4) symbolic expression.

The preceding section has roughly suggested the areas of school experience where these indigenous values are to be found. The first step in a program of moral and spiritual education is to discern them as they emerge in the school experience. As in all matters that have to do with values, this process is more of an art than a science. Discovery depends upon the sensitivity of teachers and pupils alike more than upon anything else. There is no simple and easy formula. It may be doubted that the elaborate scientific devices for measuring attitudes are of much, if any, worth in this undertaking. But teachers and pupils who develop a sensitivity for these values and cultivate the habit of looking for them will find little difficulty in discovering them.

Having discovered values, it is necessary to identify them. Otherwise they remain vague and unmanageable in that they cannot be recovered, communicated, or symbolically expressed. This identification, however, differs fundamentally from the trait approach: the process of arriving at these identified values is exactly the reverse of that of starting with traits or virtues as the end products of racial experience and imposing them upon the school experience. In this approach, the identification of values and their classification under certain categories of virtues is the result of the generalization of actually experienced values.

The process of developing moral and spiritual values is that of transforming what at the point of their origin are value potentials into actual and functioning values. This may be accomplished in part through participation in groups in which these values are operative. But more especially they need to be developed through conscious and discriminating use in reflective-purposive activities.

But the development of moral and spiritual values cannot be considered complete until they have found adequate symbolic expression. These symbols may assume many forms, such as language, art objects, the drama, the dance, ceremonials, and celebrations. By such symbolization what were vague feeling attitudes assume tangible and more or less definite forms capable of evoking the original attitudes and emotions in new situations. They also render these values sharable by particular groups and by society as a whole. They are thus caught up into the social fabric of attitudes and appreciations and become new increments in the cultural heritage.

IV

In these ways the school becomes a laboratory into which the experiences in the school itself, in the family, and in the community are brought for analysis, appraisal, and re-direction in the light of the moral and spiritual insights of mankind through countless generations in his struggle for the good life. Working on the frontier of the human adventure, where in its children and young people the human race is biologically renewed and its cultural inheritance is not only transmitted, but re-examined and augmented by new insights and achievements, the school becomes society's most dynamic and effective instrument for guaranteeing progress toward the distant goal of a better and richer human life.

CHAPTER EIGHT

A Program of Emphasis

IF MORAL and spiritual values are indigenous to the school community and the learning process and if morality and spirituality are qualities that potentially attach to each response to the situations that arise in the school community, it follows that a program for the discovery and development of moral and spiritual values should be one of emphasis integral to the total school program rather than one of additional courses or a separate department.

I

In such an approach no new subject matter is needed. This is true whether one thinks of the curriculum as having primarily to do with responding to situations or with the cultural heritage.

If the curriculum is thought of as dealing with responses to life situations, the substantive content of the learning process consists of the situation itself and of those elements that enter into its resolution. As was pointed out in Chapter V, a unit of experience consists of an identifiable situation as its *terminus a quo*, an identifiable response as its *terminus ad quem*, and the psychological processes that unite the response and the situation. If the response occurs on the reflective-purposive level there are drawn into the process of responding the resources to be found in the learner's own past experience and in the cultural heritage. The content or subject matter, therefore, of situation-response learning consists of three elements.

The first is the situation itself. It may be simple and call for an immediate reflexive or instinctive response. Or it may be complex, involving many interrelated factors of varying degrees of relevancy and requiring analysis, discrimination, and choice among a number of possible alternative outcomes.

The second element of content in resolving a given situation is the learner's own past experience. This consists of the knowledge he has acquired, his habits, his skills, his attitudes, his prejudices, and his system of values. This resource, often more than teachers realize, is of great importance in the learning process and is too much neglected or overlooked. It is a mixed resource and needs to be subjected to discrimination and criticism. Its factual knowledge is limited and often distorted by error and prejudice. Nevertheless, it is in the light of the personal experience of the particular pupil that a given situation is initially understood or judged.

The third element of content or subject matter in situation-response learning is the resource of the cultural heritage as preserved in the great traditions—the natural sciences, the social studies, the humanities, and the arts. In the traditional forms of education conceived as knowledge, this was considered the first, if not the sole, content of learning. In an experience-centered type of education such as is here assumed, the order of subject matter is reversed. Historical subject matter becomes an indispensable resource for interpreting situations and for discovering and judging their possible outcomes. In these great cultural traditions are to be found the tested knowledge, techniques, and values necessary to the most effective response to the situations that life presents to growing persons. It should be added, however, that as in the case of personal past experience, even the cultural heritage is mixed. As a record of a growing social experience it contains much incomplete and imperfect knowledge, certain provincialisms, a considerable amount of prejudice, and residual superstitions, along with a vast and growing store of verified knowledge, valid judgments of what is enduringly true and good, and tested techniques of living. Because it is a dynamic and growing tradition it needs constantly to be re-examined and revised as well as added to in the light of new and wider ranges of historical experience.

Subject matter of the situation-response type need not and cannot be introduced into the school experience. It is already there in greater abundance than teachers and administrators can hope adequately to deal with in the time and with the resources available to them.

On the other hand, if the curriculum is thought of as consisting of the cultural heritage, that also is already present in the school and, in modern times, in overwhelming abundance. So rapidly has knowledge in every field of learning grown, the best that the school can do is to select from the vast wealth of material such representative portions of the great traditions as are suited to the capacities of pupils and manageable within the limits of the school schedule.

The point, however, is that, much or little, each of the great traditions of the cultural heritage carries within itself, along with all its other priceless treasures out of mankind's cultural past, a rich deposit of moral and spiritual values. From a cultural point of view it may be said that, great as is its content of knowledge, techniques, ideas, and institutions, values—and especially moral and spiritual values—constitute its highest achievement and its most precious legacy.

It is not necessary, therefore, to "drag in" moral and spiritual values or to go out of the way to "moralize" science, literature, the social studies, or the arts. These values should be dealt with as they occur as objectively and forthrightly as every other phase of these subject matters. These values are a substantive part of man's culture and as such are self-authenticating. They are embedded in the great cultural traditions and wait only to be discovered and made explicit by teachers and pupils alike who have become sensitized to them. Unfortunately, their preparation has placed so much

emphasis upon knowledge and techniques in fields of specialization that teachers have for the most part received little
training in the discovery and development of moral and
spiritual values in their particular fields of professional
education.

II

If no new subject matter is needed, neither are separate
courses or a separate department in moral and spiritual
education. These assume an idea already dealt with, namely,
that these values are extraneous to the school and the learning process and need to be injected into them. On that
point no more need here be said.

But another consideration of major importance is that
putting the teaching of moral and spiritual values into
separate courses has the effect of uprooting them from the
rich and concrete soil of experience in which they are generated and function and of reducing them to abstractions.
Like cut flowers, they are removed from their source of sustenance and vitality and quickly wither and die. They then
become what Whitehead (*The Aims of Education*) called
"inert ideas," incapable either of interpreting reality or of
influencing life.

Moreover, such separation of moral and spiritual values
from their living context profoundly influences method in
dealing with them. The emphasis shifts from learning to
teaching. The way is set for teachers to fall into formal and
external instructional procedures.

Nor is this all. One of the more recent trends in education,
as in the sciences themselves, has been to see natural and
social processes in their interrelatedness, as in biochemistry,
astrophysics, social psychology, and cultural anthropology.
In education, below the level of graduate study and professional schools, there has been a pronounced reaction away
from free election of courses, as in early Harvard days, and
narrow specialization in particular fields of concentration to

comprehensive courses in which the various fields of culture are dealt with in their interrelatedness, as in the new Harvard plan, the University of Chicago, the general education courses at Transylvania College, and the grouping of fields at the University of Kentucky.

However important this consideration may be with reference to other fields of learning, it is especially true of values. By their very nature values are comprehensive and have their roots in a wide range of experience. This is pre-eminently the case with the revaluation of values, which is the ultimate objective of moral and spiritual education. To abstract these moral and spiritual values from the several areas of school experience in which they arise and from which they derive their sustenance and to deal with them in a separate course or department is to render more difficult the integration of values into a total meaning and worth of life, which is the ultimate ground for a philosophy of life.

III

What is indicated instead is a program of emphasis which is integral to the total program of the school. Such a program makes it possible not only to deal with these values as they emerge in the manifold relations and activities of the school community and in the subject matters of the cultural heritage, but to deal with them in their interrelatedness.

Such a program of emphasis is not the responsibility of a single teacher or group of teachers, but of the entire school personnel. Each teacher in the classroom, in the home room, in the corridors, in the cafeteria, and on the playground needs to be sensitive to these values as they emerge and to take note of them. The adviser and counselor have unusual opportunities to discover and develop them. The administrator bears a major responsibility in making possible the conditions and the atmosphere conducive to such an emphasis.

This sharing of emphasis should include in its purpose
and planning the pupils as well as teachers and administrators. In the nature of the process, the discovery and development of moral and spiritual values is not something that can
be done *to* pupils or *for* pupils. It is something that can be
done only *with* pupils. The values, precisely because they
are values, must be those of children and young people
themselves, and not merely those of their adult mentors.

On the other hand, teachers and administrators are as
much personally involved in this search for values as they are
professionally. To be effective stimulators and guides in the
discovery and development of moral and spiritual values,
they must be sensitive to these values in their own personal
experience and consciously seeking to make them operative
in their own living. The testimony of teachers who have
participated in the initial experiments of this movement in
Kentucky is that they have not only found new joy in their
work with children and young people, but are themselves
changed persons.

Such results will come not from teachers and administrators working separately in their several roles in the school,
but with a common mind and purpose through thinking,
planning, and working together to this end.

From such interest and activity there arises that subtle
and elusive, but real, something that the Greeks called
"ethos." This all-pervading spirit that gives tone and atmosphere to an institution or a group enterprise is perhaps
the greatest influence which a group exercises upon its
members. Without this ethos, no formal program, however
otherwise well conceived, can hope to affect profoundly the
attitudes of pupils.

This means that any school that would undertake a program for the discovery and development of moral and spiritual values may need to examine the values that are accepted
by it as determining the patterns of its behavior. It is not

only insincere for a school to attempt to cultivate one set
of moral and spiritual values by means of a formal program
while in its actual operations it lives by another set of values;
it is utterly useless. Such an examination might well entail
the reconstruction of autocratic rather than democratic
methods of teaching, punitive rather than remedial discipline,
dictatorial rather than inspiring administration, race prejudice rather than tolerance, and the ever-ready and uncritical
acceptance of the mores of the environing society rather than
critical appraisal and selection.

PART THREE

Techniques of a Program of Emphasis

A program of emphasis on moral and spiritual values in every phase of the school's life involves not only a different approach, but a different procedure. That procedure will consist of three basic techniques: (1) for guiding growing persons in their responses to situations; (2) for analyzing the several areas of school experience in order to discover where potential moral and spiritual values are to be found; and (3) for synthesizing particular experiences into generalized meanings and values by means of symbols.

CHAPTER NINE

Techniques of Guidance: Developing Situations

THE TECHNIQUE of guiding growing persons in responding to situations in moral and spiritual ways consists of at least four identifiable but overlapping steps: (1) developing sensitivity on the part of teacher and pupil to potential moral and spiritual values as they emerge in the process of responding to a situation; (2) identifying the values involved; (3) developing potential values into actual and operative values in the weighing, motivation, and execution of the pupil's choice of alternatives in action; and (4) giving adequate and appealing symbolic expression to the emergent values.

The specific situation will determine the order of these steps and the way in which they are taken. For example, the case of the Blue Vase, presently to be considered, starts with a symbol and works backward through the other steps. The important thing is that in guiding a growing person in his analysis of a situation, the judging of possible outcomes, and the execution of a choice of alternatives, none of these steps shall be overlooked or neglected.

For this reason, no blueprint of procedure is here suggested that can be taken over and applied in any situation. Instead, a few cases are selected from the actual school and classroom experience of administrators and teachers in the workshops and experimental schools. They are presented not because they are records of perfect handling of the cases or models of procedure, but because they are actual records of what typical administrators and teachers who were sensitive to moral and spiritual values in the everyday school experience of pupils did to develop them into effective operative values. What these educators have done, others can do in their own way in guiding pupils in other specific situations under other and different circumstances, and perhaps may do it better.

For purposes of illustration and analysis two or more cases have been selected from each of the five areas of school experience discussed in this volume. Others will be found under the analysis of the school community, curriculum content, counseling, sports and recreation, and symbolic expression.

I

THE SCHOOL COMMUNITY

The following case is selected because in a rather striking way the behavior of Mary takes place in the social setting of the school as a community in which she seeks recognition and status; because the situation has ramifications that extend beyond the school into the larger community, in this case especially the family; and because the teacher used group counseling as a method not only of helping Mary but of developing a sense of values in the group of which Mary was a member.

Mary was twelve years old. She came to school every day with stories that would have given credit to any writer of fairy tales.

At first all her friends and the teacher believed her, but when none of these stories materialized, other problems began to manifest themselves. Her friends began to turn away from her, but she only told more fantastic stories and to that added stealing and abuse of other children.

The teacher realized that Mary needed help and that the class perhaps needed a little counseling as a group. Each child was asked to write an autobiography. Needless to say,

Mary's was the most romantic of all the life stories, but nevertheless revealing in spots. One thing which Mary said was that her grandmother had come to live with them. This brought the teacher to the conclusion that such a situation might have its bearing on Mary's behavior, and she decided to visit Mary's home. Grandmother was there, though none of the affluence with which Mary had surrounded herself was present. During the course of the visit, however, the teacher discovered that grandmother had the same grandeur delusions that Mary was exhibiting in her stories. Mary adored her grandmother and was following in her footsteps.

In order to restore herself in the esteem of her friends, Mary had taken money to try to "back up" her stories of wealth and to buy favor with her friends. When this failed, she turned to abusing them by fighting and other belligerent behavior. Mary really wanted friends. She loved beautiful things and color. Her home was plain and drab; her clothes were also plain and drab. Her friends had the things she desired. Her grandmother had found a way of escaping reality and had set an example for Mary. The teacher made these deductions from Mary's life story and from her visit in her home.

With this knowledge in mind, she began counseling with her group. Stories were read and told in which it was pointed out that material things of life are not the most important factors of happiness and success. Other stories and studies, such as art, helped the group to become interested in making the best of what they had and to make the best of their homes. Friendship was stressed. Mary was assigned responsibilities which gave her a feeling of importance among her classmates. The parents were called into conference and Mary's problems were discussed with them.

Mary and her mother planned together to make their home more attractive. Friends were invited to come to their home and were made to feel welcome at any time. It was arranged for grandmother to go to Florida to spend the winter with her sister. Before long Mary became proud of what she could do rather than of what she could tell.

Even a cursory glance reveals that this situation is full of potential moral and spiritual values. Dealing with it constructively had its beginning in the sensitivity of the teacher who realized not only that Mary was much in need of understanding help, but that an important factor in the situation was the attitude of her classmates. Her resourcefulness and imagination in raising the situation into consciousness is evidenced by the clever suggestion that each member of the class write an autobiography which would bring into view conditioning factors in Mary's and their past experience and present environment. The autobiography gave an important clue in the presence and possible influence of Mary's grandmother. A visit to Mary's home disclosed the influence of the grandmother who had the same delusions of grandeur. It also disclosed the drab conditions of her home and the denial of the things that she really wanted. She had unconsciously taken over from her grandmother the mechanism of escape from reality by creating a dream world of wishful thinking. Her friends turning away from her gave her a sense of isolation and insecurity that led to stealing in order to make an impression. This case is an excellent illustration of how when one begins to analyze a situation, its relationships reach out into the wider social environment, in this case Mary's classmates and a home with an underprivileged tradition and frustrated ambitions and desires. Note also the ingenuity of this resourceful teacher in reading and telling stories that brought out in an objective way some fundamental moral and spiritual values—that material things are not the most important factors in happiness and success, making the best of what one has in improving his living conditions, and the value of friendship. A conference with her mother led to Mary's *active participation* in planning and carrying out ways to make their home more attractive, and in winning friends by inviting them to her improved home and making them welcome. The teacher also wisely saw that in accomplishing this reconstruction of Mary's behavior pattern it would be wise to change the factors in her situation, at least for a time, by making it possible gracefully

for the grandmother to spend the winter in Florida. Achievement gave Mary a sense of self-respect and justifiable satisfaction, and established her status of acceptance in the group.
This teacher had a considered technique for discovering the
moral and spiritual values of this situation and for developing them into fruitful personality results. Had she lacked
this technique, or something like it, it is not difficult to
imagine how the possibilities of this situation would have
been overlooked or mishandled. Any teacher with sensitivity,
interest in people, and imagination could do as well.

Let us examine a case of sympathetic understanding
since it illustrates in a marked manner the effect upon personality of the failure of the individual to secure recognition
and status in the school community, the concerted concern
of several of Jack's teachers and the librarian to help Jack
to a constructive adjustment, and the creative effect upon
personality development of active participation in the school
community.

Jack is sixteen years old and is in the eighth grade. He is
from a broken home. His mother and father separated and
his father remarried. Jack resents his stepmother. He has a
low I.Q. He stands almost at the bottom of his class. He
didn't seem to belong to any group. As he is rather "sissy,"
the boys did not include him in any of their activities. He
is constantly talking to one of the teachers, thus trying to
identify himself with someone.

Through the concerted efforts of several teachers, Jack was
helped to such an extent that he told one of the teachers
that this had been the best school year he had ever had.

The librarian gave much help to Jack. She asked some of
the primary teachers if they would allow Jack to have a
short period once a week in which to tell stories to the
children. Jack was made a member of the Library Club.
The children enjoyed his storytelling and were eager for him
to come each week.

The eighth-grade teacher gave him a part in a chapel program. The music teacher gave Jack a chance to play the

drum in the band. He was also placed on the school boy patrol, which gave him a sense of responsibility and a feeling of contributing to the group.

Much is still to be desired in Jack's behavior, but his adjustment is much better. He needs sympathetic understanding as much as any child I have ever seen.

The faculty working together has attempted to cause Jack to feel that he has a definite place in the school activities and that he has the interest and understanding of his teachers. The activities of the year have helped to lay the foundation for the rest of Jack's high school work.

This is an excellent illustration of the destructive effects of the isolation of the individual from the group through failure to establish normal interaction with the school community. This isolation and its accompanying insecurity began in Jack's broken home. His low I.Q. and standing at the bottom of his class had quite evidently given him a sense of inferiority. Because of his somewhat "sissy" behavior he was rejected by the other boys and was denied a part in their normal activities. There is something wistful and pathetic about his attempt to identify himself with someone by constantly talking to one of the teachers.

One notes that the concerted attempt to help Jack grew out of the sensitive concern of several teachers and the librarian over human values. Jack was not just another pupil, and a troublesome one at that, but a *person* who desperately needed understanding and help.

Note also that the method which these concerned teachers used to help Jack was through securing his participation in the normal activities of the school community at which, with his low I.Q., he could experience success. Through telling stories to the children at a regularly scheduled period, through membership in the Library Club, through a part in the chapel program, through playing the drum in the band, and through taking responsibility on the patrol—in these ways he came to think of himself as a real person rendering a real service to the school community and receiving an honored status because of his contribution to its ongoing life. It must have meant much to him to discover that the children were eager for his storytelling hour to come.

II

CURRICULUM CONTENT

From all the areas of curriculum content, let us select two—one from the teaching of general science and the other from the teaching of mathematics.

Let us examine this case reported by a teacher of general science:

As a result of our beautification work on our school lawn, various groups began to take field trips. For the lower age groups this started with a trip around the schoolyard where they began to learn the names and locations of the trees and shrubs, and following this with the important facts that these very plants have much to contribute not only to individual well-being, but to the well-being of the larger world. At various seasons these trips were repeated.

After the children made these trips in their own schoolyard, they planned trips in their community, and thus had the opportunity to compare the plant life of the community with that of the school grounds. They were becoming conscious of the wonders of nature as evidenced by the various leaves, seeds, and twigs they brought home. They not only brought plant life, but were beginning to bring animal life. This made a learning situation for the teachers and the necessity of an emotional adjustment because they never knew what would be brought in next.

A third-grade child's father sent in a magnificent specimen of a hornet's nest, and the child was given the privilege of taking it to every room in the school for all to share.

A fourth-grade child became interested in guppies, and so a lady in the community sent the child a pair. The class did much research on the life and habits of guppies. The children did reference work and reading, and soon they watched eagerly for "Mrs. Guppy" to have her babies. When this time arrived the children were thrilled, but life dealt unkindly with the mother because she died before all of the babies came. Seeing the children's disappointment, the teacher wisely dissected the female and showed the children the embryo fish. They were so pleased to have had this opportunity that they took them to the principal for her to see. Thus, they had witnessed both birth and death. They were not discouraged, for later they secured another pair of guppies along with a few snails, and it was not long before they were the proud foster parents of guppies.

One of the third-grade teachers visited the South and brought a cotton ball and some cotton seed back with her. She shared the experience of this trip with her class by telling them about the trip, about the cotton fields, some of the many uses of cotton, and its part in our existence. The children wanted to know if they could not plant the cotton seed and see if they could raise cotton. They prepared the soil and carefully planted the seed, and before the year was over their efforts were rewarded, for they had a cotton plant with real cotton on it.

Another group of children had become interested in the study of bees, a highly complex society; so they asked if they might have an indoor hive. They enlisted the interest of a bee society, and through this interest they were given a bee hive. Under the direction of a member of the bee club they learned how to care for bees. They read much about bees, and this hive was an inspiration to the group for the whole year, for they were actually seeing the wonders of nature unfold before them.

It is evident from the manner in which this case is reported that the teachers had become sensitive to the value potentials in the teaching of science. Note also that they began with the specific and concrete situation in which the children found themselves. They started with them where they were in their interaction with the natural world, rather than with abstract generalizations from a science textbook. From this beginning point they helped the children follow the ramifications of their initial experience of nature in the schoolyard out into the community and the larger world. Note also that

the children had firsthand experience of the objects of nature
—leaves, seeds, and twigs which they observed, handled, and
brought home. Through such sensory contacts they began
to acquire a "feel" of the wonder of nature. Note also the
use of the children's "leading-on" interests from plant to
animal life and the growing of cotton, reaching its most intimate and vivid expression in relation to the guppies and
the complex society of the bees.

It would be difficult to imagine a more delicate and wholesome introduction to the biological processes and mysteries
of birth and death than in their loving care of "Mrs. Guppy"
and her babies.

Moreover, the entire experience took place in a group
situation, involving not only the children themselves but
the father who brought in the magnificent hornet's nest, the
bee society, and the lady who gave them the guppies.

Another significant aspect of this learning situation in
science was the actual use of experimentation in the care of
the guppies, the planting of cotton, and the care of the bees.
Still another was the way in which the children, their interest
aroused by a stimulating sense of need for knowledge, searched for it where it might be found—in reading books about
guppies and in consulting a bee expert.

Some of the values that were discovered and developed
in this firsthand experience of nature were an appreciation
of the orderliness and dependability of nature's laws, the
reverence-inspiring mystery of life in nature, sharing a newly
discovered knowledge in a co-operative enterprise, and a
sense of responsibility.

Since it is often assumed that moral and spiritual values
have little or no relation to the teaching of mathematics,
let us consider this case reported by a mathematics teacher
and her evaluation of it:

During the first week of school, the arithmetic class of the
eighth grade organized a store for the purchase and sale of
school supplies to teachers and pupils. Each of the twenty-

seven children was given a specific job in the store. Twenty of them became salesmen for the twenty classes of the school. Their duties included the writing up of orders and the delivery of supplies to the respective rooms. In addition to the salesmen, one child had charge of the stock on hand and of ordering new supplies; two were appointed to act as cashier and assistant cashier; two were given the task of filling orders; one became bookkeeper; and one became treasurer.

Each morning, each class, when supplies were needed, sent a child to the eighth grade with a list of supplies needed and the money to pay for them. The child went directly to his salesman, while the regular work continued with little or no heed paid to the children coming into the room. The salesman accepted the orders and put them aside until store time.

At the appointed time the salesmen prepared their order sheets and took them to the cashier. The cashier checked the sheets, made corrections, counted the money, and made change. Each salesman took his order to the stock supply where the orders were filled. The salesmen then delivered the orders to the classrooms and returned the order sheets which bore the signatures of the respective room representatives. After the cashier had received all the returned order sheets, a total of sales was made by grades and items.

After the daily sales summaries were made, the bookkeeper entered the totals in the journal and the student in charge of stock made a record of each sale in the stockbook. This furnished a perpetual inventory which the stock clerk used in preparing his orders.

The project yielded the following values: (1) Financially, the store was a success, with a profit for the year of $300.00. (2) Educationally, it provided opportunities to develop skills through school experiences which are continuous with real life problems. From the standpoint of human relations, it developed such desirable traits as accuracy, honesty, neatness, and promptness. Its success depended upon maintaining good human relations among staff members and with the customers throughout the school. (3) The project led directly to an understanding of various operations involved in banking. All bills were paid by check. All stubs in the checkbook were kept. The class visited the bank where they learned something of the way in which it is operated. (4) Other business principles were also involved. The class learned firsthand how to figure discounts. The children liked the storekeeping. Actually selling merchandise, ordering supplies, handling money, making change, banking, figuring discounts, and paying bills are real experiences continuous with adult life outside the schoolroom.

III

PERSONAL AND GROUP COUNSELING

As an illustration of guidance in personal counseling, let us consider this case of cheating reported by an eighth-grade teacher:

It was reported to the eighth-grade teacher by the children that Charles was cheating to get his good grades, and that they were doing their work honestly and getting the low grades; therefore they felt that something should be done about this. The teacher talked to Charles about this cheating, but he vigorously denied the accusations. On the next test the same thing occurred, and the teacher then took her problem to the principal. It was decided that Charles' mother should be called in because the teacher and the principal felt that undue pressure at home was being put on the boy. After failing to get in contact at the time with the mother, the teacher asked the principal to help her with Charles. The principal told him that he had been accused by his classmates, and she wondered if he would mind taking the test over and prove to them that he had not been cheating. The teacher had sent the questions to the principal and the test was given. Since Charles was sitting next to the principal's desk, it was easy to check if he was cheating.

He wrote some of the answers and then took a piece of paper from his pocket and copied the remaining one. When questioned by the principal about this cheating, he was not embarrassed except to the extent of what he was going to tell his mother about why he had not received an A. The school continued to work with Charles, and in a counseling session he began to talk about what he did at home, and we then learned that he was concerned with making money in his spare time because of the fact that in case his father died he would have to care for his mother; therefore he must get grades and go to high school. He said that his brother had always gotten good grades, so that it was unnecessary for him to cheat in order to pass to the next grade. Thus, with the cause removed, there was no longer necessity for cheating. The principal had assured him that it was not necessary for him to cheat in order to pass to the next grade. When questioned about his father's health he stated that his father was quite well. We had previously sent his report home stating that he was doing failing work, and it was that action that caused the mother to contact the school.

When we told her about Charles' cheating, she was more concerned about his failing and immediately wanted to take the few recreational privileges away from him so that he could have more time for study. We asked her not to do this because Charles needed these outlets, and we knew at school that he was working up to his mental ability. We also told her that Charles would be promoted, and thus for this year the problem of Charles' cheating was solved.

The procedure used in this case illustrates well one type of personal counseling that attempts to see and understand the counselee in his social situation and to take account of factors in his environment that influence his behavior. Furthermore, it seeks to change the factors in the environment in such a way as to effect a satisfactory adjustment. In this instance the mother was chiefly to blame in placing upon the son with a low level of intelligence a burden of expectation and even pressure beyond his ability to bear. He was also under a sense of pressure from the fact that his brother had always made good grades. There was also a sense of anxiety arising from the fact that if his father should die, Charles would have to provide for his mother. His mother's chief concern was not with understanding Charles, but with her embarrassment that he got poor grades.

In this case the teacher and the principal understood that before a satisfactory adjustment could be made it would be necessary to examine the causes of the behavior and remove or change them. The principal made it clear to Charles that he did not have to have high grades in order to pass to the next grade. The fact that his father was shown to be in excellent health went far in removing the source of Charles' anxiety. When it was made clear to Charles that no more was expected of him than his ability would justify, the pressure of striving for an impossible goal was relieved. An understanding of the dynamic nature of personality was evidenced by the insistence by the principal and teacher that Charles' activities be not taken away, but utilized more constructively as a means of self-fulfillment. One wishes that it had been possible to follow this case through to see what the long-term results were in his subsequent behavior and attitudes, as was not possible within the time limits of the experimental school to date.

Of a different type of counseling is the unguided interview. The following recorded interview is a good example of this technique:

Lucy: (Smiling as she walked into the room) Hello, Mrs. H. I thought I would come in and see you a few minutes.

Teacher: I'm glad you came. Won't you sit down?

Lucy: Maybe you don't have time to be bothered with me. It seems nobody else does.

Teacher: It makes me very happy that you wanted to come to see me. (Pause—several seconds of silence.) You felt that you had something to talk with me about?

Lucy: Yes, I just thought I'd come in and see what you thought about something.

Teacher: You wanted to see what I thought about something?

(More silence.)

Lucy: Uh-uh—Do you think I'm old enough to go to see a show that's coming to Lexington called "Mom and Dad"?

Teacher: You think you would like to see the show that is called "Mom and Dad"?

Lucy: Yes, I want to see it, but Mama just has a fit when I mention it.

Teacher: Your mother feels that she doesn't want you to go to that kind of show?

Lucy: No, I don't know why she acts as she does when I want to go anyplace—Yes, I do too know why, I think.

Teacher: You feel that you understand why your mother objects.

Lucy: Yes. It's because Myrtle stays home and never wants to go any place and she thinks I ought to be like her. Just stay at home and work and never go any place.

Teacher: I presume Myrtle is your sister.

Lucy: Yes. Everybody says we look alike, but I don't think so. Her hair is blacker than mine; she doesn't act like me. Seems like I just want to go some place all the time.

Teacher: You like to have fun.

Lucy: My goodness yes, but I don't have much; they won't let me. Mama said that show wasn't fit for a married person to see, let alone me. But it just seems I want to see it. Myrtle doesn't want to see it.

Teacher: You talked with Myrtle about going to see it and she doesn't want to go.

Lucy: No. I knew there wasn't any use.

Teacher: That might be one way you could get to go yourself—to persuade Myrtle to go with you.

Lucy: I can't do that because she won't.

Teacher: You tried it and you think she won't go.

Lucy: I haven't asked her, but I know she won't. I don't have any patience any more.

Teacher: You don't think you have any patience.

Lucy: No, Mrs. A knows that.

Teacher: You think Mrs. A thinks you haven't any patience.

Lucy: You know what I said to her the other day?

Teacher: You don't mean you lost your patience with Mrs. A.

Lucy: Yes, I did. She helped somebody to cut out their skirt and wouldn't help me and I told her that girl ought to have a good skirt and she wouldn't help me.

Teacher: You feel that you wanted to hurt Mrs. A's feelings because she wouldn't help you.

Lucy: Yes. I did, but I didn't want to.

Teacher: You think you hurt her feelings.

Lucy: No, because the next day I felt bad about what I had said and I thought I would tell her I just lost my patience and was sorry, but when I went in the room she didn't act mad at me and she helped me every time I needed it.

Teacher: You felt happy when you knew Mrs. A wasn't angry with you.

Lucy: Yes. But you know one thing. Sometimes I think Mrs. K doesn't like me. She's not always friendly.

Teacher: You feel that there are times when Mrs. K doesn't act friendly toward you.

Lucy: Yes, she looks at me and smiles sometimes and then the next time I see her she doesn't have a word to say or anything.

Teacher: Mrs. K has so many pupils I guess she is kept pretty busy trying to smile at all of them.

Lucy: That's what I mean, I don't have any patience—I guess it is just me. I'm just like that. Miss G doesn't talk very much to me. I guess she likes me, though.

Teacher: I'm sure that Miss G is interested in you.

(Bell rings.)

Lucy: Well, I have to go. I'll come back and see you next week and talk to you about the show. I didn't get to tell you about Mrs. S.

Teacher: I'm glad you came.

Lucy: I'll be looking for you at this time one day next week.

Note that in this type of counseling the initiative rests entirely with the counselee. Note also that the counselee is thrown back entirely upon her own resources for the formulation and solution of her problem. The counselor contributes nothing to the interview but the opportunity for the counselee to bring to the conscious surface her own inner wishes, attitudes, frustrations, the statement of her problem, and her groping for a way out. There is no attempt on the part of the counselor to explore the social situation out of which the problem arises, no attempt to help the counselee to rearrange the factors of her environment, no attempt to direct the counselee to sources of information that would be of help to her.

Some adjustment problems are better dealt with in an objective and impersonal way through group counseling. Let us take the case of Jim and the homeroom teacher from type experience (4) in the listing on page 121: understanding and adjusting to the personal and social aspects of sex.

Jim, aged seventeen, came to the office of his homeroom teacher early one morning and told the following story:

"Miss Blossom, two of my friends and I are in trouble. When I was fifteen I spent the summer in Des Moines and I dated a very nice girl. She never did anything that made us think that she would do anything wrong when we took her out. I got a letter from her yesterday, and she wrote me that she was going to have a baby, and said that one of us was its father. She said that her father would see to it that one of us married her. Now, I know that none of us got her into trouble, and I also know that I won't have to marry her because my dad can pay her and her dad any price. I'm not worried about me, but I am worried about my two friends because one of them might be forced to marry that girl, and they are no more guilty than I am. I would like to know how a boy can tell when he is and when he isn't dating what he calls a nice girl. Could we discuss dating, necking, petting or whatever we want to call it at our homeroom meeting this afternoon?"

Boy-girl relations were discussed at that homeroom meeting and at three successive homeroom meetings. The boys and girls suggested the following causes might result in the problem mentioned by Jim: the way the girls dress; "grownup" feeling; ignorance of the consequences; no sense of values; drinking; no self-respect; no respect for others.

The boys and girls suggested that such problems could be prevented if the following understandings and values were developed: understanding of and appreciation for our bodies; understanding of the value of a sound mind and body; acceptance of others for what they are; concern for the welfare of others; appreciation for others; spiritual need for a desirable sense of values; sense of direction for spontaneous behavior.

It is significant that this problem was not injected into the experience of these high school students by someone who wanted to teach a lesson on sex behavior, but grew up out of the actual experience of members of the class who were sensitive to this problem and wanted help in solving it. There are some matters, notably in such an area as sex, that can better be discussed in an objective and impersonal way rather than in a subjective and personal manner. The intensity of interest in this problem is evidenced by the fact that its discussion was prolonged through several sessions. Under the guidance of the wise homeroom teacher the students themselves sought out the causes that might lead to the situation in which Jim was involved. Under this same wise guidance the students themselves explored ways in which such situations could be avoided, and it is especially noteworthy that the students felt that the best way to prevent such situations from occurring would be through the cultivation of moral and spiritual values. It would be impossible to imagine a case in which these values are more involved.

IV

SPORTS AND RECREATION

The following case illustrates how games may be used in developing a sense of personal integrity:

The game of "Steal the Bacon" was being played by the second grade. The children were divided into two equal sides, with lines facing each other and the children having corresponding numbers on each side. An Indian club was placed midway between the lines. The physical education director called a number. One child from each side tried to steal the club. If he got back to his team safely with the club it meant a point for his side, but if he were touched by his opponent it would mean a point for the other side.

On this occasion Jerry had the club and carried it to his side. Both sides claimed the point. It was difficult for the director to judge whether Jerry had been touched or not, and so she asked him. Of course it meant the point would go to his opponents, but Jerry immediately said, "Yes, I was touched."

The director stopped the game, got the attention of everyone, and praised Jerry for being honest. He received recognition at the proper time. It made him proud that he had done the right thing. The children were all impressed by the recognition that he had received.

Note that in dealing with this situation this second-grade teacher showed confidence in Jerry by putting him on his honor and assuming that he would tell the truth, even to his own immediate disadvantage and that of his side. Jerry's honest reply shows that there is in most persons a fundamental integrity that can be evoked and depended upon if the situation is handled rightly, and this would seem to be a better attitude for teachers to take than expecting wrong behavior. An important part of the technique of this teacher is that she immediately gave public recognition to this honest behavior. This gave Jerry a sense of recognition for having done right—a satisfaction that spread to the entire group, whether winners or losers. The recognition was full compensation, or more, for the loss of the point by Jerry's side. On that day the value of integrity was immensely enhanced in the whole second grade.

This case illustrates the possibility of developing values through making of decisions in an athletic situation:

One of the teachers realized that when disputes arose on the playground she was called upon to settle them, and the children would abide by her decision. She felt that this was not teaching any values in good sportsmanship or in living together. So she told the children that she would like for them to settle their own disputes, such as whose bat it is, whether a child is out, and about what position the children would play when they had a ball game. She told them why an umpire was needed, and that they must learn to make their own decisions.

This worked well with the exception of two children who seemed to feel that everyone was against them. When things were not settled in their favor they would lose their tempers and quit playing, regardless of the game.

The class talked this situation over with these boys, and told them that they were going to try to help them. One interesting fact was that the two boys recognized their problem. As this procedure progressed there was a notable change in these boys. By learning to accept decisions on the playground they were also learning to make and accept decisions in the classroom.

Bobby in particular was quite belligerent in the beginning, but was soon taking much pride in himself when the children would tell the teacher that Bobby didn't get mad today and Bobby, who had been quite unhappy most of the time, was beginning to be a happy child. He was learning to admit that he was wrong. He was learning to share, and the school was taking on a new meaning for him. It was no longer a place to which he had to come. Bobby's home life was not happy.

The attitudes that he had built up at home and had brought to school were gradually disappearing. Not only was Bobby happier, but the children and teacher had the satisfaction of seeing a job well done.

Through understanding the functional relation of values to experience, this teacher had learned that values cannot be transmitted from teacher to pupils by talking about them or by exhortation. To be real and vital they have to grow out of experience and function in experience. These values the pupils learned by making decisions for themselves.

One of the most interesting aspects of this case is the illustration of the way in which social participation changes the behavior of the individual. Bobby was unco-operative at first and even belligerent, losing his temper when he did not get his way. But through the other boys going out of their way to help Bobby and through his participation in a socially minded and co-operative group, Bobby, having come to realize his problem, was learning to accept decisions and to co-operate.

Note that Bobby's home life was not happy, and he brought his resentment and rebellion to school. But note also that in finding satisfaction in co-operation and friendliness Bobby began to be happy and to enjoy rather than avoid school. Note also the enriching satisfaction that came to the teacher from seeing these values emerge and grow under her hand. No wonder that one of the teachers in the experimental schools said that she had found a new happiness and self-fulfillment in her teaching as a result of her effort to discover and develop moral and spiritual values!

V

SYMBOLIC EXPRESSION

One of the loveliest illustrations of how a symbol can express, communicate, and enrich meanings and appreciations that came out of the experimental schools is the case of the Blue Vase.

In a medical settlement in the mountains where grew laurel, rhododendron, ferns, evergreens, and many other specimens of natural beauty, there lived a teacher, a woman doctor, a nurse, and a seventeen-year-old mountain girl who helped with the laundry and chores. She milked the cow, washed the dishes, swept, and dusted. Each day while dusting, the girl commented upon a blue vase that sat on the dining-room table. One day the owner of the vase said, "June, I know that you like my blue vase and I am going to give it to you under one condition: you are to promise that you will keep it filled the year around with something that grows in these mountains. If you will look around, you can always find something beautiful here."

Here is the case of a girl growing up against the background of a drab, isolated, and underprivileged mountain community. But as helper to a teacher, doctor, and nurse, she is brought into contact with people from the larger outlying world of activity, culture, and humanitarian interests. With eyes made sensitive by a richer cultural inheritance, they "saw" beauties in the world of nature that were hidden from the eyes of the girl because her cultural background

had not awakened her to perceive beauty and wonder in the
exquisitely beautiful objects of her native mountain home—
laurel, rhododendron, ferns, evergreens. Seeing them daily
in the blue vase as she went about her menial tasks and per-
ceiving how much they were appreciated by the teacher, the
doctor, and the nurse, the blue vase came to be associated
with beauty, and admiration was evoked in her heart. Seizing
upon this interest, the owner of the vase used it as a means of
stimulating insight into and appreciation of the beautiful
things that were to be found everywhere about the mountain
girl.

It is regrettable that the account of this intriguing illustration of what a symbol of beauty can do in the appreciation
and, perhaps, if we knew all the consequents, in the creation
of beauty could not be followed through its later developments. But in any case the Blue Vase filled with lovely mountain flowers did more to create a sense of beauty than any
amount of talk about beauty or precepts could do. That is
the nature of symbols. And by this experience of beauty, a
drab and unseeing self has been stimulated and enriched.

Among the various art forms—painting, music, sculpture,
architecture, poetry—the drama has been one of the most
effective media for the expression of meanings and values,
for their communication, and for their recovery from past
experience. Here is a particularly appealing case from a
class studying American history in one of the experimental
schools:

"Thanksgiving 2000 A.D."

Act I

The scene is Thanksgiving eve. Father, mother, and the
two children are discussing plans for the coming Thanksgiving holiday. Father and son are bickering about the desirable location of seats for the football game. Daughter is
completely engrossed in her personal appearance, and informs
the family in no uncertain terms that she "wouldn't be interested in going anyplace with any of them." Mother is

planning a Thanksgiving bridge party, and is only interested in getting the remainder of the family out of the house. Grandmother suggests that they might all go to church. The suggestion meets with no success because she is quickly informed that they do not have time, the preacher is a bore, and the right sort of people no longer attend their church. Then the scene quickly becomes one of confusion, because a bevy of friends descends upon them. Mother, the boy, and the girl disappear, and father is left to entertain the men. During the course of their conversation it is pointed out that they are opposed to freedom of the press (if it differs from their viewpoint), freedom of speech, D.P.'s (foreigners) entering the country. Finally the visitors leave and the family drops off to sleep. A shadowy figure enters the scene. The figure tells grandmother (who is wide-awake) that he is the Spirit of Thanksgiving. He is going to show the family what Thanksgiving would be like without the values they are so unappreciative of today. She agrees with him, and he slowly leads the group in a trance from the stage.

Act II

Instead of the attractive, cozy living room in Act I, we see a bare stage. The only furnishings are a table and four chairs, a weird machine, and a picture of "Big Brother." An unearthly light shines upon the four people seated at the table. They are eating a Thanksgiving dinner which consists of dried seaweed, meat pills, a cherry pie. The latter is dispensed from the machine and must be eaten, because it is Big Brother's favorite dessert. Each remark is uttered with fear because of the new police listening device which has just been installed. The new car, which had to be purchased because the Traffic Manager demanded that they do so, is discussed. Someone makes the unfortunate remark, "Why can't we go to church?" and the police descend. The family is marched to jail on the charge of criticizing the government.

Act III

The family has awakened from its dream. They look around them and contrast their unrecognized freedoms with the nightmare they had just experienced. They discuss how they can spend a happy, congenial day by going to church, eating dinner together, and then attending a football game. Their plans are completed, and the play closes with a radio softly playing Thanksgiving hymns.

In this case, instead of seizing upon some already existing symbolic expression of the spirit of Thanksgiving, the class out of its own awakened insight and resources creates its own symbol for a suitable expression. The pupils themselves work out the script, arrange the scenes, furnish the cast, and present the play. Consequently, the drama is alive with meaning, as the reader is likely to feel on reading it.

It is interesting to note that the drama makes use of a symbol to bind together and fittingly express what it has intended to show—the soft playing of Thanksgiving hymns. In this selection of hymns, the group reached out into another great cultural tradition—that of religion as expressed in its liturgy.

The school in which this drama was produced has an art laboratory in which one may see young students absorbed in creating beauty through the media of painting, modeling, ceramics, textile weaving, designing. This school has demonstrated that, however precious the already existing artistic forms, it has, under the stimulating guidance of imaginative and resourceful teachers, unlimited capacity for the creation of indigenous art forms. What this school is doing, any school with resourceful and sensitive leadership can do on a scale commensurate with its resources.

In the analysis of the techniques used in the development of these situations, they have not been criticized because they did not always end with a symbolic expression. The reason for this is that symbols grow out of generalized values in which many specific situations are involved. To strain after a suitable symbol in every specific situation would distort the use of symbols and in many cases render them mechanical, unreal, and unconvincing. Perhaps, as in the case of teaching general science, a suitable poem celebrating the wonders and mysteries of nature might have been used, or perhaps, as in the Spirit of Thanksgiving, one of the great hymns of the church, such as "This Is Our Father's World" or, with older children, Haydn's "Creation." It is as easy to overdo the use of symbols as it is to neglect them. It must be left to the sense of fitness of a sensitive teacher to decide what is best to do under the circumstances.

CHAPTER TEN

Techniques of Analysis: The School Community

I

THE FIRST necessity in the discovery and development of moral and spiritual values in the school community is the development of awareness of the school as a community on the part of administrators, teachers, and pupils. The frequently all but exclusive emphasis upon subject matter in formal education has tended to obscure this awareness. When it is fully realized that it is through the process of socialization involving group status and roles assumed in group relations that growing persons achieve selfhood and that it is through the harmonious integration of these many and often conflicting roles that one becomes a mature person, the school as a community of interacting persons assumes primary importance in the development of wholesome personality. These values are integral to the warp and woof of existence and grow directly out of group experience. Viewed in this light, the school is not merely a preparation for life, but is life itself. Neither are moral and spiritual values mere listings of abstract virtues, but the dynamics of a value-judging approach to living.

Moreover, the school is set in the larger community of which it is a part. The things that the community values enter into the life of the school and condition it. Sometimes they support what the school is trying to accomplish; sometimes they are in conflict with it. This lays upon the school the responsibility not only of helping children to understand their experience in the community, but of developing discriminating attitudes toward the ends and behaviors that are operative in the environing community.

Within the larger community the school itself functions as a community. It involves the intimate and continuous interaction of persons and groups in the manifold relations and functions that make it a community. Like the larger community, the school derives its spirit and tone from the values it accepts and the patterns of behavior it sanctions. In view of the great educational influence of accepted values in the school community, the social analyst should be concerned to discover what the dominant interests of the school community are. Since boys and girls cannot well learn what the life of the school contradicts, an attempt to develop moral and spiritual values may in some instances require a reorientation and reconstruction of the attitudes of the school itself.

The social analysis of the school community and of the behavior situations involved in its experience calls for two types of technique. The first has to do with the discovery and comprehensive listing of behavior situations. The second has to do with the analysis of behavior situations, once they have been discovered, for their factors and possible outcomes as a basis for helping children and young people as well as teachers to discover and develop moral and spiritual values in these situations.

II

Once administrators, teachers, and pupils have become fully aware of the school as a community, a technique will need to be devised for the discovery of behavior situations through organized observation, description, and record. Experience has shown that unless such observation is directed carefully, the results will be superficial and selective. Only the obvious and that which is abnormal or tends to disturb the orderly processes of the school will be perceived. This is well illustrated by the following case:

The fourth-grade teachers of a city school system were asked to observe and record the behavior situations of their pupils. They were an intelligent and co-operative group of teachers. When, after a considerable period of observation and recording of pupil behavior, their reports were tabulated, they showed a narrow range of pupil behavior, chiefly concerned with infraction of rules, tardiness, cheating, discourtesy, disorder on the playgrounds and in the halls, and other like forms of behavior that are annoying to the teacher and

DISTRIBUTION OF BEHAVIOR SITUATIONS

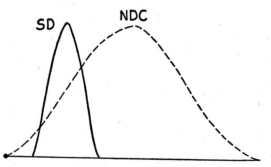

Fig. 5 Selective distribution of unorganized observation. NDC, the theoretically normal curve of distribution had all the instances of behavior been observed. SD, the highly selected distribution resulting from unorganized observation.

disrupt the orderliness of the school community. Strikingly lacking were instances of normal behavior in the fulfillment of the normal relations and functions of the school community. The selective results are represented in Fig. 5.

This is an excellent illustration of the need for a thorough social analysis of behavior situations in the school community. The highly distorted and unsatisfactory results of mere collecting of cases were not due to the intentions of the teachers. They were intelligent, co-operative, and impressed with the importance of the purpose of their observation. The fault lay in the failure to use a technique of observation that would insure a fair distribution of all types of pupil behavior, normal as well as abnormal. By looking at behavior situations en masse, they saw little, and that little was chiefly abnormal and unrepresentative. They were not sensitive to the great range of areas of experience represented by the normal curve of distribution.

In order to avoid this error, the author devised a technique for narrowing the field of observation over a wide spread of relations and activities so as to get a balanced and comprehensive listing of behavior situations. This technique consists of making a crosshatch of personal and group relations on the one hand and the major areas of school experience on the other, thus:

	Person to person	Person to group	Group to person	Group to group
Administration				
Teachers				
Curriculum				
Classroom				
Home room				
Cafeteria				
Playground				
Corridors				
Social organizations				
Musical organizations				
Athletics				
Dramatic organizations				
Physical education				
Fine art activities				
Home-school relations				
Etc.				

After the fields of observation were thus narrowed, each was viewed through five successive "screens"—(1) Activities (working, thinking, play, etc.), (2) Psycho-sociological Factors (customs, beliefs, tradition, public opinion, fashion, etc.), (3) Use of Time and Property (schedule, money allotment, food, clothing, furnishings, automobile, playgrounds, tools, etc.), (4) "Wishes" (for recognition, social response, security, new experience, self-expression, etc.), and (5) Miscellaneous (seeing another's point of view, group pressure, conflict of loyalties, alibis, superiority or inferiority complexes, etc.).

The use of this rather simple device, which any school can adapt to its situation, with senior high pupils in a metropolitan city resulted in the listing of some 4,000 identifiable but overlapping behavior situations. Upon analysis, these yielded 21 types of experience which teachers and parents may look for and in which a rich content of value potential is to be found. For such help as they may offer teachers as a check list in discovering the behavior situations of their pupils they are given here: (1) Achieving and maintaining physical health and fitness; (2) achieving and maintaining mental health; (3) participating in the educational process; (4) understanding and adjusting to personal and social aspects of sex; (5) participating in the economic order; (6) choosing and engaging in a vocation; (7) utilizing leisure time through avocation, recreation, amusement; (8) appreciating and creating beauty; (9) achieving a religious adjustment to one's world and participating in religious activities and institutions; (10) fostering the interpenetration of cultures through encouraging racial friendship, international understanding, adjusting economic differences, and sharing religion; (11) developing and maintaining friendships; (12) participating in group government; (13) adjusting to the social group by accepting or rejecting mores, standards, and public opinion, and by achieving a place in society; (14) preparing for and sharing in courtship, marriage, parenthood-childhood, family relations, and family-community life; (15) understanding and controlling impulses; (16) exercising and adjusting to authority; (17) facing the issues of war and peace; (18) caring for pets and animals; (19) exercising and responding to leadership; (20) behaving toward those considered less or more fortunate; (21) building and testing a philosophy of life.

III

A second technique concerns the analysis of behavior situations, once they have been discovered, for their factors and possible outcomes as a basis for helping children and young people to discover and develop moral and spiritual value potentials in these situations. This technique follows the general pattern outlined in Chapter V. It involves getting the facts, the location and definition of the central problem involved, the identification of value potentials, and the working out of effective educational procedures for dealing with the situation in the light of its moral and spiritual possibilities. In this it has been found useful to diagram the situation. When this is done, it will frequently be found that the primary relation, such as that between pupil and teacher, involves numerous other conditioning relations, such as those with the family, other pupils, and membership in school and community groups.

IV

The following cases, selected from the experience of the experimental schools, will serve to illustrate in some degree techniques of dealing with situations.

Pupil-Teacher Co-operation. In view of the fact that at one time or another children become ill and miss a great deal of school, this case is used to show how a teacher and a class concerned themselves about a member of the class.

One of the girls in my home room had been absent for a few days, and when no one seemed to know the reason for her absence, two of her friends decided to go to her home and see her. Her mother had been dead several years and an older sister was trying to keep the family together. I was told that her father drank a great deal. Her older brother, who was in the twelfth grade, did not live in the same home and did not seem to know much about his sister. There was another girl of junior age in the family.

In our room it is a custom to send flowers or a gift to any of the group who became ill. The girls who had made the visit were very much distressed over the conditions they found. The father had not thought it necessary to have a doctor. The room was rather bare and the girl's pajamas and bed were not clean. It was decided that we should buy pajamas, and then it was found that there was also enough money to buy a few toilet articles. Some of the other teachers became interested, and one of them took the matter to her church school, which adopted Betty and her sister.

When Betty came to school she seemed happy because so much had been done for her. She began to take more interest in her appearance. The other girls seemed to take more interest in her, too.

Betty was given economic help and made to feel that others were interested in her.

Her classmates gained experience in doing something to meet the needs of others and in sharing things they had.

The other teachers and the church group concerned were brought to feel the responsibility of helping one less fortunate.

Personal Security. Many children in our schools today lack the feeling of security that is so essential to their well-being. All teachers should be alert to this problem and develop techniques to deal with situations in this connection. One teacher handled such a problem in the following manner.

Susie was seven years old. She was in the first grade. She was a diabetic and had to take insulin each morning; therefore she was listless and unable to concentrate on her work. This made it difficult for her to read or write. She demanded much attention from the teacher. She did not know how to work independently.

It seemed that Susie's mother was not sympathetic. She did not seem to understand how much her child needed security and sympathetic understanding. Yet, when the teacher talked with her about Susie's difficulties in reading, she would say, "Yes, I know that sometimes Susie reads fairly well and at other times she can't read at all."

Susie felt so insecure that she would touch the teacher each time she came near her. Often during the class she would reach for the teacher's hand. The teacher would hold her hand and try to make her feel at ease.

The teacher talked with Susie's mother and as a result the child was not only taken to a physician for further treatment, but also was given a little more help and understanding at home.

Through thoughtfulness on the part of the teacher Susie was not called upon on the mornings when she was not so well. Much love and care was given to the child, and thus by the end of school her adjustment was much improved.

A Problem of Health Insecurity. The basic problem of health, so acute in our communities, may cause a situation that affects the entire group as well as the individual. This case illustrates a behavior problem caused by poor health and how its successful treatment helped the climate of the classroom.

Howard was a little boy in the first grade. He was seven years old but small for his age. He had bad tonsils and as a result was absent from school forty days during the year. When he was in school he took no part in the activities of his room. He did little of his written work. Seemingly, he had no interest in anything that was taking place in school. He was quite listless. He just sat and watched the other children. The children recognized the fact that Howard did not do his work or participate in group activities.

Toward the last of the school term, Howard had his tonsils removed. When he recovered, his attention and his attitude were indeed changed. He began to take a small part in the activities of the room.

The teacher felt that he needed to feel himself a part of the group, and so when the time came to present an assembly program for the elementary grades, Howard was given a place on the program. He took a small part in the dramatization of the Good Samaritan.

What seemed an insignificant thing gave to this child a feeling of satisfaction, a feeling of belonging to the group, and the joy of being commended by the other pupils. The child's adjustment was much better and his participation in the activities of the room increased.

Security in the Group. In every person is an inherent desire to experience some success. It is the teacher's concern to draw out the good qualities in every child. This giving of one's self and sharing of talents gives one a sense of belonging; thus security is established. The following case shows where a teacher brought out the child's positive values and minimized the weak ones.

Billy is one of my slower students in reading and spelling. He is a good worker, however, in the fields of science and art. While others were reading bird stories and writing information for our nature book, Billy was selected to make the cover for the book. He also had some interesting information about chickadees. Instead of struggling with spelling and writing as was his experience in the past, he dictated his story to me and I acted as his secretary and wrote it down just as he had given it to me.

Heretofore, he had lost interest because of his difficulty with spelling and writing. When he had experienced success, he had the feeling and knowledge that he had made a worthwhile contribution to the making of our nature book.

Talent Appreciation. Here is a case of how discovering what a child can do successfully provides a key for resolving a self-destroying frustration.

Dick is in the first grade. He is eight years old and is large for his age. He has a slight speech defect. He is pale and appears to be undernourished. He came to our school from California. This is his second year in the first grade. He was antagonistic. His attitude toward the other children was poor. He was ready to fight at "the drop of a hat." He seemed to be bristling all the time. But at the same time he was the most forsaken-looking little boy that I have ever seen. He couldn't seem to find his place in the group, and time after time he annoyed someone, tripped a classmate, or had a free-for-all fight.

I discovered that Dick had unusual talent in art. I immediately began to use that talent to give Dick a feeling of satisfaction. I praised his work. I showed it to other children and other teachers. I asked him to illustrate many of our reading charts. This he did well.

Reading was difficult for Dick, and as soon as he had become better adjusted I began to talk with him about improving his reading. I told him that he was a good artist but that an artist needed to know how to read and that I wanted him to make his reading as good as his drawing.

One day the junior high mathematics class had an exhibit of simple figures that the children had drawn and colored. The teacher of the class invited Dick to see the exhibit. He seemed to get much pleasure from this experience.

By now Dick was really trying to read well. Quite often he would forget and do unkind things in the room and on the playground. I talked with him and told him I needed his help with some of the younger children.

I also assigned him some jobs in the classroom that gave him a feeling of responsibility. I called him my helper and continued to praise his art work.

By this time Dick's attitudes were so much improved that I could hardly realize that he was the same frustrated little boy that had entered the class in September. I talked with Dick's mother a number of times. She told me that she could see a great change in his attitude and behavior.

Through Dick's talent I had found a way to help him find security and satisfaction, and a desire to do other things better.

The Handicapped Child. In all communities at one time or another a handicapped child enters the school and presents a problem.

A little boy enrolled in kindergarten. He was physically handicapped, wearing braces and using crutches. His parents co-operated with the teacher, principal, and superintendent. All persons were consulted and reached an agreement on steps toward the solution of the problem. It was agreed that the parents would be responsible for bringing their son to the schoolroom and coming after him at the closing period.

The little boy had a bright and cheerful disposition and created a rich field for moral and spiritual values. He needed assistance in sitting down. One child held his chair firmly while he sat down, and put his crutches against the wall. The children took turns doing this, and also in hanging up his wraps. The little boy was mentally bright, loved music, and participated in the classroom activities. He, in turn, was able to perform little duties such as passing napkins and holding the flag while the others saluted.

The teacher commented on the willingness of the group to accept him as one of them, their willingness to assist him, and the joy they seemed to receive in helping him. They definitely had sympathy and not pity for him. The instructor said too that he contributed something that she or the others did not have. The children learned thoughtfulness and consideration for someone less fortunate than themselves.

Making Choices. Everyone has to make decisions, great or small. Sometimes we must sacrifice our wants for the group. We must learn to make proper evaluations. Here is how one teacher brought this to the attention of the children.

Last year a third-grade teacher asked the children if they would like to have some time all their own to do with as they wished, so long as they did not disturb their neighbors. Naturally, they were delighted. She gave them the opportunity to think over what they might like to do. Some chose to read, others to finish up art work, still others to study spelling, and some wasted their time. When the free period had ended, the teacher asked the children how they had spent their time and to share this information with the class. One child had been reading about rocks and told the children what he had read; another told a story; still another showed the picture he had drawn.

A discussion followed. Questions were asked: Would they like to continue this type of "choosing activity"? Was it worthwhile? Did they use their time wisely? Do they think they will use it to better advantage next time? Each time the free period was given, the teacher noticed a marked improvement in their tastes and a decrease in the number of idlers. It was suggested that each child make his own chart and head it, "Things I Do in My Free Period."

Natural Resources. The child's relation to nature involves much more than such information as he may gain through formal study. It involves a personal relation to it and responsibility for the conservation of its priceless resources. The following case illustrates how one teacher went about establishing these attitudes.

One group of children after studying about conservation became much interested in the drainage problem in one part of our schoolyard and on the playground. They asked if they might not do something about this, since this was their yard and they saw this need. The teacher readily went to work helping them plan their program. They called in a conservation expert who went over the area with them and made suggestions about what could be done. After he made his suggestions, this group visited a farm that had had extensive work done on it to correct erosion. With this in mind they came back to the school to solve their problem. They asked a neighbor across the road if he would bring his tractor over and disk a field for them. They planted the balanced mixture of grasses for this type of erosion. Soon after these seeds were planted we had many hard rains, so that the stand of grass was not good. But they were not discouraged. This spring they repeated the process. They also made a brick wall in the back of the baseball backstop to stop erosion. Quite often they would check this wall, and if any bricks were loose, they would replace them.

We believe that many results will follow in the future from this experience. We felt that the project had many values such as: (1) a concept of the universe as logical, orderly, and predictable; (2) sharing talent, material goods, and responsibility; and (3) a feeling of responsibility to other individuals, to the group, and to the community.

CHAPTER ELEVEN

Techniques of Analysis:
Curriculum Content

THE CURRICULUM, whether it is concerned with the cultural heritage or life adjustment problems, is a fertile field for the discovery and development of moral and spiritual values. This is particularly true when the curriculum is thought of in terms of its functional relation to the life process. It then becomes a sequence of experiences which grow out of teachers and learners working together on individual and group concerns of everyday living. So understood, the curriculum is designed to do more than pass on the cultural heritage from one generation to another. It will give children and young people experiences which will help them to meet persistent life situations successfully and to improve the quality of social living. The cultural heritage is utilized as it contributes to the understanding and control of present-day personal and social needs as they appear in the latest phase of the human adventure.

A preliminary analysis of the curriculum currently in use in the Kentucky schools, made by the groups working on curriculum content, yielded the following list of potential values: (1) experiencing some degree of achievement; (2) respect for the rights, opinions, and property of all human beings; (3) sacrificing some individuality for the welfare of the group; (4) making choices and value judgments; (5) a concept of the universe as a logical, orderly, and predictable place; (6) honest personal relationships; (7) an open-minded, critical, and inquiring attitude; (8) sharing talent, material goods, and responsibilities; (9) sympathy, understanding, kindness, and a feeling of warmth toward one's fellow men; (10) justice for all; (11) obedience to laws; (12) personal survival; (13) a feeling of responsibility to other individuals, to groups, and to the community; (14) wanting to get along with others; (15) respect for the dignity and worth of every human being; (16) recognition of the dignity of all kinds of productive labor and services; (17) loyalty to one's group; (18) anticipation of the consequences of one's acts in the lives of others and of one's self; (19) treating values as relevant to the situations in which people find themselves rather than as absolutes; (20) belief in some creative guiding power higher than man; (21) integrity of thought and act.

In dealing with these values, account should be taken of the fact that they are frequently in conflict in our society. When this is the case, the school should help the pupils to identify and clarify the values they hold, to see their social implications, and through new experience to examine and revise them. Neither are these values to be sought primarily in crisis situations, but in normal, day-to-day contact with the curriculum. Furthermore, it should always be remembered that quite apart from any formal technique in dealing with these values, teachers influence pupils in developing values through their own behavior, their treatment of curriculum content, and their personal attitudes.

The values listed above are, of course, generalized values, and are useful as an over-all check list. But in order to realize the full value content of the curriculum it is necessary to analyze each subject field for its specific and unique value potentials. For this purpose the group broke down the curriculum into those subjects that have to do with the cultural heritage and those that have to do with life adjustment education. The heritage subjects fall under: the humanities (language, music, art, literature) ; the social sciences (history, geography, civics, economics, social studies, problems of democracy) ; the natural sciences (astronomy, geology, chemistry, physics, biology, physiology) ; and mathematics (arithmetic, algebra, geometry, trigonometry) . The life adjustment subjects fall under vocational exploratory areas (agriculture, industrial arts, commercial subjects, home economics, health, physical education) . What follows is the result of the analysis of the major subject fields of the school curriculum.

I

HUMANITIES

Language. A language program will provide for impression and expression. Through impression it should seek the enrichment of the child's experience; through expression it should seek to develop the attitudes and skills of communication. Specifically, its objectives should be:

1. The enrichment of the content of experience through: a wide range of first-hand experiences; well-chosen vicarious experiences; the use of new words gained from experience; group experiencing, group sharing, and group responsibility; listening to and evaluating with discrimination various art forms; the assimilation and organization of ideas through skillful guidance and questioning.

2. The cultivation of skills and expression through: creation of the desire for expression by developing a social atmosphere; providing situations that call for different forms of expression (talking over plans, sharing, reporting, writing invitations and letters, etc.) ; providing audience situations that encourage sticking to the point and clearness of speech; developing concern for accuracy and form through written expression.

3. The development of social attitudes and practices through: cultivation of habits of courtesy, attentiveness, and responsibility; using generally accepted forms of greeting; taking one's turn; enjoying give-and-take conversation; welcoming kindly criticism of teacher and classmates.

4. The development of skills in voice control and correct usage that make for effective oral expression.

Foreign Language. Language is man's most universal medium of communication. It is primarily concerned with meanings and judgments about experience. Different races and nationalities, however, have developed different language forms for recording and communicating their experience. Foreign language is thus the opening way into the thought and life of other peoples.

1. The study of foreign language opens to the pupil the way to an understanding of a vastly wider range of experience than that of his own group or time, and thus tends to break down narrow provincialisms and prejudices. It helps to make one a citizen of the world.

2. It makes quite obvious the interdependence of nations and cultures in their total approach to reality.

3. It helps the pupil to appreciate the contributions of the various peoples to man's total culture.

4. Too often foreign language is taught as a formal discipline in vocabulary and grammar, rather than in its functional relation to communication. In the former case foreign language tends to be a dead subject; in the latter case it is alive with interest and meaning because it is the medium which man has invented through his long cultural history for the recording and communication of his experience to his fellow men.

Music and Art. As esthetic forms, music and art are in themselves types of valuational experience. As such they sustain a close relation to moral and spiritual values. Whether in the form of art appreciation or of creative art, both music and art are replete with moral and spiritual values.

1. In their forms of appreciation both music and art provide insights into other cultures and periods of history. They are, therefore, fruitful media for the understanding of other peoples, races, and cultures and of the contributions they have made to civilization.

2. In their creative aspects, music and art are vehicles for the expression of one's highest ideals and subtlest emotions. Music and art, like literature, are concerned with the in-

terpretation and criticism of life. In either case they are value judgments about life. As contemplation and appraisal, they are somewhat removed from raw experience and therefore stress the more spiritual content of experience. Both are essentially idioms of the spirit—a wordless language which is universally understood. This is doubtless why religion through the ages has turned to music and art as media for the expression of its profoundest feelings about life and its meaning. For this reason also the greatest return comes from experiencing music and art rather than verbalizing about them. They are self-authenticating and carry their own meaning and value. Those who have listened to great music or contemplated in rapt wonder great paintings, great sculpture, or great architecture know how true this is.

3. In both hearing music and viewing art, there is need for discrimination and value judgments between that which is noble and enduring and that which is trivial and vulgar. Through such discrimination the teacher has the opportunity of helping the pupil to develop true judgments regarding the true, the good, and the beautiful.

4. In music ensemble groups, such as orchestras and choral associations, there are abundant opportunities to develop co-operation, understanding, and oneness of intention and act at the highest esthetic level.

5. Musical activity is too often restricted to a limited group, whereas opportunity should be given to all to participate in collective performance.

6. In both music and art, appreciations and skills may be developed that will carry over into adult life as avocational activities of sustained and sustaining interest.

7. Songs and art objects can be used to illustrate the contributions which the several races and cultures have made to man's growing appreciations and thus make for understanding and good will.

Literature. Literature as a subject area holds great promise for the development of moral and spiritual values. The stuff of literature is the stuff of the sociologist and of the philosopher—man's relation to God, to his fellow man, and to himself. These ideas are presented by the true artist in a form that is more easily assimilated and more directly influential upon the reader because they emerge from personal and intimate experience of specific human situations presented with the "sharpness and intensity of art."

1. The great promise of literature lies in the fact that it: shows forth the glory of God; illuminates the dignity of man; provides a sensuous and emotional fulfillment; presents a sense of beauty of form, tone, and style; presents an approach to life; develops an image of people working out a common fate; deals with human relationships, such as a young man coming to understand himself, adjustment to young love, resolution of a family conflict, a person involved in racial intolerance; deals with discrimination and choices; shows that all men are involved in a web of relationships; substitutes a frame of mind that seeks to understand rather than to blame; helps the reader to put himself in another's place through sympathetic imagination; provides a wider perspective than the reader's age or group can provide; helps to see life in significant patterns and causal relationships; helps to form the personality of the reader by making him aware of the fact that in terms of his own bent he can accept or reject pressures, can choose one line of behavior rather than another, and can reinforce or modify his environment; gives the reader a sense of the validity of his own personal response to life; helps the reader to assimilate the cultural pattern of his group.

2. The teacher of literature needs these understandings: that literature exercises its greatest influence on the emotional level; that literature must be experienced to have appreciable influence upon the reader; that values do not come through mere information but through additional experiences; that literature should deal with the concerns of the reader; that real reading experience is a complex, unstereotyped, never to be duplicated combination of book plus the reader; that under certain conditions many contemporary works may be of far greater value to a given reader than the classics; that literature has social origins and social effects; that literature read just for fun is perhaps the most influential of all reading; that the teacher himself must experience literature before he can help another to enter upon this great adventure.

3. Some approaches which may assist the teacher in helping pupils to derive from literature those moral and spiritual values which it promises are: know the concerns of the individuals and the group; discover the readiness of the reader for the materials (vocabulary, reading skill, powers of attention, emotional development, experiences, needs) ; select materials on the basis of the learner's past experience and emotional level; provide a wide range of reading materials and let the child choose; talk honestly with the reader or group about what has been read, recognizing the validity of the reader's response, exchanging reactions, and explaining the setting and author's viewpoint; analyze the content in the light of its values, human relationships, and character delineation rather than in the light of factual presentations; base oral and written compositions on real life situations and moral issues, thereby providing opportunities for pupils to clarify and express attitudes and value judgments; through discussion enable the student to gain the full meaning of what the author is trying to express; help the student to interpret and evaluate the author's communication and to incorporate it into his own set of meanings.

II

SOCIAL SCIENCES

The social sciences present many opportunities for the discovery and development of moral and spiritual values. The following listing will give some idea of the richness of this field:

1. Among the values of the social studies may be suggested: the content of the social studies provides many experiences that help pupils to discover the essential principles of democracy; the world is a place of many races, cultures, creeds, and occupations and each has contributed to our civilization; through materials dealing with current events and controversial questions the pupils may develop awareness of significant events and appraise them critically; an understanding of the continuity of history and the relevance of developing ideas to the modern world; sensitivity to the antisocial values involved in the careless exploitation of natural and

human resources; the understanding of the situation of minority groups and the recognition that democracy demands respect for the rights, privileges, and dignity of all members of society; the widening of perspectives from the earliest grades up; an appreciation of the place of such institutions as the family, the church, and government bodies in the community.

2. The social studies should offer experiences that will help the pupil to deal with present social situations as well as to understand the past and thereby develop such values as: appreciation of the country's past; faith in our country's and the world's future; understanding of the present; self-control; a realistic attitude toward change; a constructive attitude toward the operations of government; a world outlook and understanding; recognizing and evaluating the changing concepts of man's relations to his fellow men and God; a belief in the potential value of man; the possibility of achieving good will among men.

3. One of the most fruitful ways of arriving at an understanding and appreciation of America's past is through entering into the experiences of its leaders, the situations which they faced, and the ideals they stood for.

4. An examination of our cherished documents, such as the Mayflower Compact, the Declaration of Independence, Lincoln's Gettysburg Address, and the messages of the Presidents, may be used to bring out the standards which have inspired faith in the American adventure.

5. An understanding of the relation of the present to the past may well start with a study of situations near at hand, such as: the soil and its contribution to the development of the community; conditions with regard to races, minority groups, public services, industry and labor groups; comparison with living standards of other countries; and discussion of controversial issues without propaganda.

6. The social studies offer an unusual opportunity to develop in the pupil a constructive attitude toward change.

7. An understanding of the operations of government may be had through observing these operations in the local community, the state, and the nation by visits to governmental agencies and noting that their effectiveness depends upon justice, honesty, and courtesy.

8. The growth of moral and spiritual ideas is revealed in the changing conceptions of the relation of man to God and of man to man as found in the evolving experience of different times and peoples.

9. The social studies emphasize the results of social participation and group action.

10. A study of the United Nations offers many opportunities for projects of inquiry into and discussion of the ideals that underlie the Charter as an instrument of a better life for all mankind.

III

NATURAL SCIENCES

Contrary to a widely held notion, science, both in its results and in its method, presents a particularly fruitful field for the discovery and development of moral and spiritual values, especially because it plays such a dominant part in modern life. Not only does science as a method involve ethical qualities of the highest order, but its results have far-reaching social, moral, and spiritual consequences.

1. Science teaching should lay the foundation for cause-effect thinking and should replace superstition with fact. It may well result in a concept of a creative force at work in the universe. It leads to a concept of the universe as a logical, orderly, and predictable place. Science gives the pupil understandings necessary to achieving a satisfactory adjustment to his environment. Its method gives an opportunity for the development of reflective thinking, intellectual honesty, open-mindedness, and suspended judgment. It affords an insight into the interdependence of natural phenomena. Laboratory projects offer rich opportunities for co-operation, courtesy, initiative, and personal integrity. Its findings provide factual insight into the problem of race. It provides the necessary information for personal and community health. The method of science provides a procedure for dealing with the problems of everyday living. Science makes clear the relation of natural resources to the quality of life among a given people. Teachers should emphasize the fact that science exists for man, not man for science.

2. In addition to regular classroom and laboratory procedures, field trips are productive of value appreciation. Among the wide variety of field trips may be mentioned trips to identify and classify animals and plants, visits to museums and zoological and botanical gardens, trips to caves and other natural phenomena, visits to industrial plants, observation of heavenly bodies, observation of the causes and results of erosion, visits to engineering projects, telephone buildings, aeroplane fields, radio stations, and power plants.

3. A fruitful source of values in the field of science is the study of the lives of great scientists and their achievements, such as Pasteur, Galileo, and Edison.

4. Elementary science, which is not pursued as separate fields, offers one of the chief means for the integration of learning for the young child. Thus, when a child learns to grow a flower from a bulb, he learns simultaneously many things, such as the conditions of growth, the dependability of nature, the place of human intention and care, the enjoyment of beauty.

5. The seasons offer many opportunities for activities in elementary science. Those followed in one school for winter —watching the changing sky, making evening sky maps, studying a snowflake, setting up a simple weather station, befriending winter birds, comparing range of foods, holding a winter flower show, tracing the activities of animals—will illustrate what any resourceful teacher can do.

IV

MATHEMATICS

Also contrary to a widespread impression, mathematics offers a rich vein of moral and spiritual values to the teacher who is sensitive to them. Life in most of its aspects is quantitative. Mathematics is the device which man has created for dealing with the quantitative aspects of his experience.

1. The teacher of mathematics should keep in mind as guiding principles the use, where possible, of actual life situations, the function of mathematics as an instrument for understanding the processes and structure of the universe,

and the development in the pupil of the ability to make sound judgments in respect to quantitative problems.

2. Arithmetic in the home offers an opportunity to see how money should be spent in relation to personal and family needs, the dishonesty of living beyond one's means, the need for sharing with others, responsibility for sharing in the family income and expenditures, and the unwisdom of buying on credit or installment.

3. The arithmetic of banking may be so taught as to show the value of thrift, an appreciation of savings accounts, of how through compound interest consistent savings become large amounts, the value of credit and financial reputation, the danger and extravagance of becoming involved with a loan company.

4. The arithmetic of the community and state emphasizes the obligation of the citizen for services rendered him, an understanding of the methods of collecting taxes, duties, and revenues, and the necessity of honesty in respect to tax evasion, smuggling, and hidden assets.

5. Social arithmetic emphasizes the importance of insurance as protection to one's self and others, the importance of saving for old age and sickness, the desirability of not being dependent upon society or others, and the social responsibility of employer and employee to each other.

6. The use of mathematics in representing facts should stress honesty in representing facts and the development of a critical attitude toward statistics which are often used to distort facts, as well as graphs which are most useful when properly used but misleading when wrongly used.

7. The arithmetic of measurement should point out the relative nature of measurement to different kinds of data and the fact that exact measurement is impossible.

8. Intuitive geometry may develop appreciation of form in commonplace objects like the silo, flower beds, cable of a bridge, a crayon box, a tennis court. It may point out the fact that "God eternally geometrizes," as evidenced in the cylindrical forms of tree trunks, the curve of the circle, the elliptical paths of the planets, the conical shape of a pile of sand or coal, the perfect form of the quartz crystal and snowflake, and the symmetry of the animal and human forms. It may also show the beauty in modern design of the machine, architecture, and textiles.

9. Algebra stresses the importance of accuracy, the formula as a means of expressing relations, and the power to generalize.

10. Demonstrative geometry may develop capacities for original thinking, logical thinking, the rejection of irrelevant facts, as well as an appreciation of the beauty of form.

11. As a science, mathematics stresses eternal truths in mathematical form, functional relationships, and a broad conception of the vastness and order of the universe.

V

VOCATIONAL EXPLORATORY AREAS

Perhaps vocation more than anything else influences the development of personality. If chosen under wise guidance, it makes possible the development of one's characteristic interests and capacities, while at the same time it provides the avenue through which one makes his contribution to the common good. Its choice and pursuit, therefore, lies close to the central core of personality.

1. Agriculture provides the opportunity for intimate contact with the soil and the processes of growth. It should lead to an understanding of the necessity of working in accord with the laws of nature. It offers an opportunity for something creative and a sense of co-operation with the creative forces at work in nature. It provides a foundation for respect for natural resources and a concern for their conservation. It should emphasize the source of food for the maintenance of the human race.

2. The industrial arts offer an opportunity for the development of an appreciation of good workmanship and design, together with pride in one's work. They encourage one to finish what he has begun. They stress the necessity of personal industry and of that personal integrity that will bring out the character of the material with which one works and the character of the craftsman. They afford opportunity to develop respect for property and tools. If wholeheartedly and skillfully pursued, they give the satisfaction of creative beauty.

3. Commercial education affords to pupils the opportunity to develop habits of neatness, accuracy, responsibility, initiative, co-operation, and conservation of materials. It affords a basis for the understanding and practice of good employer-employee relations. It gives to the pupil a sense of participation in the complex process of production, consumption, and exchange.

4. Home economics emphasizes the nature and importance of the home as the primary social unit. It brings to light the relations and responsibilities of persons living together in face-to-face association. It affords an opportunity to interpret marriage and the rearing of children in their ideal significance. It elevates homemaking to the level of a noble vocation. It emphasizes the orderly arrangement of the house, good taste in furniture and decorations, a carefully planned budget, and the amenities of intimate association. It offers opportunity for creative expression in food, homecraft, clothing, furnishings. It emphasizes in an unusual way the need for personal and group loyalty and a deep sense of dedication.

Health and Physical Education. Health and physical education fall in the area of life adjustment education. Since learning in this field is directly concerned with life situations, its value content is more obvious and immediate. Teachers in this field have unusual opportunities to help pupils discover and develop moral and spiritual values.

1. Health and physical education programs should lead to a respect for the body and wonder at its delicate and complex nature.

2. Health and physical education should lead to mutual respect and wholesome boy-girl relations through an understanding of the nature and functions of sex.

3. Health and physical education should develop an appreciation of and effort to achieve physical and mental fitness.

4. They should create attitudes and habits that will carry over into adult life.

5. They afford an opportunity to understand the responsibilities of parenthood and family life.

6. They should make it possible for children and young people to accept temporary or permanent physical handicaps

CHAPTER TWELVE

Techniques of Analysis: Counseling

W<small>E ARE</small> coming to see that education is concerned with the normal growth of the whole person in relation to his natural and social world and not, as so often has been thought, exclusively or primarily with basic knowledge and skills. Also, among the major discoveries of modern psychology has been the fact of individual differences and the social nature of personality. As a result, increasingly the objective of education is coming to be thought of as the development of the wholesome personality of the pupil in the light of his unique interests and capacities and in constructive adjustment in his social relations.

The group working in this area sought to come to agreement on certain basic principles of guidance, to explore and experiment with various techniques, and to assemble some representative cases that might serve as useful illustrations of procedure in dealing with adjustment problems.

I

The group agreed that a guidance program, of which counseling is a major part, should be based upon the assumption that the school exists for the pupil. It was also agreed that while teachers may give individual counseling, there should be an organized and concerted effort on the part of the entire staff and that this may best be brought about by making the pupil aware of permanent values that will enable him to make proper adjustments and wise choices as he meets new situations and problems in the school experience. Also, there is no one technique of counseling, since each counselor is a unique individual dealing with unique personalities. Above all, counselors should guard against the danger of imposing their own values upon the counselee rather than assisting him to recognize his own ability to solve his problem.

On the assumption that moral and spiritual education is that phase of the school program that seeks to help growing persons achieve an understanding of their relations to nature and society, learn to control their conduct by these standards, and develop a philosophy of life, the task of the counselor is to help the pupils meet the challenges of life as they exist in an increasingly complex social order. Counseling is to be thought of as a process of freeing one from his own emotions and helping him to find his own answer to his problem after he has recognized his own need.

On the basis of these assumptions, the group outlined nine principles for the guidance of a counseling program:

1. All persons have values. Perhaps some of these are not socially accepted, even though they may dominate their behavior.
2. Values cannot be taught verbally. Values develop as the result of experience.
3. Values, feeling, purposes, goals are major determinants of behavior. Social or group pressure may cause undesirable behavior and be the means of influencing the formulation or acceptance of values.
4. Feelings, purposes, and goals are fairly permanent traits in people, but can be changed.
5. A person has within himself the potential ability to meet his own problems. We must remember that his problems are not our (adult) problems.
6. To free this ability the counselor employs certain techniques that will help the person to view his problem in a new light and make adjustment to life situations.
7. The main agent of change is the attitude of the counselor. His attitude must be one of deep understanding and warmth toward the counselee. He must accept the counselee

as an individual who has the right to be as he is or to change
if he chooses to do so. There must be permissiveness and
understanding.

8. The center of the counseling process is on present
feeling, not past. The analytic approach has no place in
counseling.

9. Limits are necessary. Such limits may be helpful where
few are possible, when they are clearly defined in the mind
of the counselor, when they are stated as parts of the situations but not as a directive from the counselor, and when
they are not dwelt upon.

II

Most, though not all (as for example, in the case of physical health), adjustment problems have their origin in social
relations. It is helpful to counselors, therefore, to be aware
of the areas in which maladjustments are likely to arise.

The Symonds and Jackson study of some 175 cases in the
New York City schools lists the following sources in the
order of their frequency:

In relation to home and family	36
In relation to other pupils	33
In relation to teachers	33
In relation to curriculum	24
In relation to the social life of the school	23
In relation to administration	14
In relation to personal affairs	12

Dr. Roy A. Burkhart's study of behavior situations in the
Hyde Park High School of Chicago brought to light the
following areas from which adjustment problems arise: group
acceptance or rejection, boy-girl relationships, family relationships, pupil-teacher relations, vocation, conflict of group
mores, and educational guidance.

The list of twenty-one types of behavior situations resulting from the Analysis of Behavior Situations of High School
Young People as given in Chapter X will serve counselors
as a useful guide as to where to look for maladjustments.

III

Guidance in the school should be concerned primarily with helping pupils to achieve normal adjustments in their relationships and with preventing adjustment failures. It is, therefore, of great importance to be able to detect the signs of adjustment failures. Certain overt behaviors are symptomatic of deep-lying causes of maladjustment. The wise counselor will not be content to deal with the symptoms, but will use them as means for discovering the causes of the maladjustment, often deeply hidden and unconsciously concealed.

There are a number of fairly well-defined behavior patterns maladjustment, often deeply and unconsciously concealed.

1. Withdrawal, as shown in shyness, failure to participate in normal group activities, the wearing of a "mask" for protection against criticism. Underneath there are frequent turbulent emotions that erupt into uncontrolled laughing or sobbing.

2. Evasion, as evidenced by unwillingness to face the facts in the situation or the issue involved.

3. Escape, in which one experience, often imaginary, is substituted for the unpleasant experience by daydreaming or by deliberate flight into some other and more agreeable kind of experience.

4. Compensation, in which one unconsciously attempts to make up for a felt deficiency in one direction by an exaggerated behavior in another direction.

5. Aggressiveness, as when one who feels himself not to measure up to social expectation or to be disapproved assumes an overactive attitude which is frequently antagonistic or boorish.

6. Attitudes of inferiority or superiority.

It cannot too strongly be emphasized that when the exploration of these and other symptoms reveals a pathological mental state, the case should be referred to a professional psychoanalyst or psychiatrist.

IV

Two types of counseling are appropriate to the school: individual counseling and group counseling.

The techniques of individual counseling will depend upon the relative emphasis placed upon an inquiry into the conditioning factors of the environment and upon positive guidance, or upon the capacity of the counselee to manage his own situation with his own resources without recourse to an objective examination of the conditioning social factors. The former assumes the form of a case study, the latter the form of the unguided interview.

Those who emphasize the importance of environmental factors will use something like the following technique:

1. Establish rapport with the counselee.
2. Get at the essential facts preceding and surrounding the situation through a case history, records, tests, and the interview.
3. Attempt to get at the configuration of the personality of the counselee.
4. See the counselee in the context of his environment.
5. Listen without shock or condemnation.
6. Help the counselee to locate and define his own problem.
7. Help the counselee to arrive at his own solution.
8. Shift the environment when necessary and possible.

Those who emphasize the ability of the counselee to solve his problem with his own resources without recourse to a consideration of environmental factors depend primarily upon the unguided interview in which:

1. The counselor waits for the counselee to seek him out.
2. The counselor seeks to create rapport by assuming an understanding and warm response to the counselee.
3. In the interview itself, the counselor waits for the counselee to take the initiative throughout, even remaining silent through long periods of time on occasion.

4. In his responses, the counselor repeats, perhaps in a somewhat different form, what the counselee has said, without adding any new ideas or giving any direction to the conversation.

5. Normally, the counselee brings the interview to a close, perhaps by suggesting another interview.

Perhaps the counselor will regard neither of these techniques as exclusive, but will, in the light of given circumstances, combine them.

Group counseling, on the other hand, approaches the individual through group participation. It works through the media of the home room, the common learning class, self-governing groups, clubs, and so forth. Its techniques consist of:

1. Identification with the group.
2. Building group morale.
3. Group consideration of problems.
4. Group enterprises.
5. The constructive organization of group pressure.

The following cases illustrate various types of counseling situations and procedures.

A Case of Stealing. Billy had never stolen until he became a fifth grader, and quite often money was beginning to disappear after he had been around it. The teacher became suspicious of Billy, and the next time money disappeared she took Billy to the office. Through the combined efforts of both the teacher and the principal Billy admitted that he had stolen the money for an older boy who had spent his lunch money to go to the show the night before. In order for Billy to keep the boy's approval, he admitted that he had been stealing for quite a long time. The teacher counseled with Billy about stealing and its complications and also the kinds of friends a person should select. Billy seemed to understand and said he would not steal again.

One day the fifth graders saw a film together, and the boy with whom Billy had been sitting told his teacher that his lunch money was gone. Immediately the teacher felt that

Billy had taken the money, even though the boy with whom he had been sitting was his best friend. Billy's teacher had the same feeling, and the two of them took him to the office of the principal. Billy said that he had not taken the money; in fact, he had not taken anything since his conference with the teacher. There was still a doubt in the minds of these adults about Billy's veracity. Later the child who reported his money stolen said that he had found it in another pocket. It was then that these adults learned moral and spiritual values. They also realized that irreparable damage had been done to this child, and that even apologies that were made could not undo this damage that had already been done.

A Case of Vocational Counseling. Since we have a new school, we have just scratched the surface so far as setting up a vocational counseling program is concerned. We do have the beginning, however, of what we hope will be a good program. After administering a series of tests to our pupils near the end of the school year, our pupils are permitted to fill out subject choice sheets for the following school year. This is done in the home room under the guidance of the teacher who has been with that particular group of boys and girls for a whole term. After the home room teacher has checked the selections, the pupil then will go to the subject-matter teacher who counsels and approves the choices made by the pupils.

The Employment Service of the Economic Security Department administers a general battery of tests to determine the aptitude of the boys and girls of grades eleven and twelve. After the tests are scored each pupil is interviewed by experienced counselors from the Employment Service. Here students are helped to see in what fields they probably would succeed and are guided into the various fields of work.

Pupils are also given tests of their aptitude in more specific fields. The Clerical Aptitude Test is one example of what is provided by the Employment Service free of charge to the school. Pupils are interviewed after the tests have been scored, at which time the interviewer discusses the outcome of the tests, the subjects which the pupils can use to increase their skills in this field, and how to prepare for a future career.

Teachers, with the help of the librarian and pupils, collect books, magazines, and clippings of job descriptions for use in learning about the various fields of work. These materials are used by classes in several subject-matter areas. Many films are used in all subject-matter classes that show something of the nature of the jobs in several of the occupations.

To say that this report is a clear picture of what we are doing in the way of vocational counseling would not do justice to our whole school effort in this area. Pupils confer with individual teachers and the principal about what they would like to do after graduation. These conferences are informal in nature and may take place in the classrooms, in the halls, on the school grounds, or in the homes of teachers and pupils.

Our obligation as teachers does not end at graduation of the pupil. For many this is the point where the pupil comes face to face with a problem and needs help in making a decision. Phone calls, letters, and personal visits by the pupil to the teachers and principal are ways in which the pupil seeks help in making a decision.

We realize that our program is not good enough. We have accomplished what we have in just two years. From having attended the workshop and having been inspired by our experience, we feel that we are in a better position more efficiently to direct our boys and girls in their effort to find their choice of a life work.

A Case of Principal-Parent Counseling. One morning the teacher came into the office and said, "Mary's mother and father have separated and she is living with her father. Her sister is living with her mother." This immediately posed not only a school problem, but a community problem as well. A day or so later the teacher reported that the father had left home and the police were looking for him. When we went home from school that afternoon, it was easy to understand why the police were looking for him, since he had rated the front page of local newspapers by his behavior. Since this man was a patron of the school, the school felt that it was part of the principal's duty to help work out this situation. That very day Mary's teacher had reported to the principal that Mary had hit a little boy in the mouth. Up to this time Mary had never exhibited any such behavior.

Having known the father much better than she knew the mother, the principal anticipated a visit with him. Needless to say, he came rather sheepishly and apparently much in need of friendly counsel. The principal joked with him about his conduct, and at the same time tried to get it over to him that he had an obligation not only to his children, but also to his wife. The principal discussed with him the incident of Mary hitting the little boy, and it was explained that this behavior that Mary had exhibited was probably due to her feeling of insecurity and divided affection. This filled him with remorse as he began to realize the effects of his conduct on the child. Following this he readily discussed his problem and expressed his feelings quite strongly concerning his children. The principal knew that he was genuinely fond of his children and that he often assumed the role of the mother as well as that of father, since the mother did not have the same interest and was rather timid. Following this conversation, the father requested the principal to talk with his wife, which she gladly consented to do.

A few days later the mother came to school, and the story of Mary's behavior was related to her by the principal, who assured her that she did not wish to pry into their private lives, but was deeply concerned about what effect this might have on the children. After listening attentively to the story about her children, the mother presented her problem and expressed her feelings about the whole affair.

Our job at the school was to effect a reconciliation, but at the same time to give these parents the feeling that they were doing it themselves. With the school taking the role of "go-between," it was not long until this family was united. When they left for a two-weeks vacation in Florida, the teachers and principal felt a deep sense of satisfaction in knowing that they had had a part in helping this family solve its problems.

CHAPTER THIRTEEN

Techniques of Analysis: Sports and Recreation

SINCE physical education was dealt with under curriculum content, the present chapter will be concerned only with sports and recreation.

The educational value of play has long been recognized. It was an integral part of Greek education. The modern appreciation of play as a medium of education, however, began with Froebel in the early part of the nineteenth century. With the increase of leisure time under the conditions of modern industrialization, the importance of play in its various aspects has assumed vastly greater proportions, particularly as a fundamental objective of education, not only in the constructive use of sports and recreation during the school experience, but as preparation for the constructive use of leisure time in after-school years. If constructively used, it offers a greatly extended educational opportunity. On the other hand, if left undirected, the increased amount of leisure time is a source of personal and social danger.

Great as are the opportunities in sports and recreation for education in general, they offer especially fertile fields for the discovery and development of moral and spiritual values. In many ways they are for the pupil the most vivid and appealing forms of experience in the school community. The situations involved in sports and recreation are particularly loaded with adjustment problems in which moral and spiritual attitudes, standards, and behavior patterns are involved. These situations are real, immediate, and concrete and therefore far removed from abstractions, generalities, and merely verbal precepts. They present action situations in which values are intrinsically involved rather than carried over from other learning situations.

I

As compared with many other types of school experience, sports offer unusually favorable opportunities for the cultivation of such traits as:

1. Honesty.
2. Co-operation.
3. Loyalty to the group and to the tradition of a sport.
4. The merging of one's self with the group in purpose and action for a common objective.
5. Physical health and fitness for reasons that are immediate and convincing.
6. Appreciation of and respect for the body.
7. Discipline which in a large measure is self-imposed for a desired end.
8. Courtesy.
9. Losing as well as winning gracefully in accordance with the ideal of "good sportsmanship."

On the contrary, as often happens, sports present unusual dangers when these values are neglected or violated. This is why athletics may be a grave problem in education and sometimes gets out of hand. Some of these dangers are these:

1. The limiting of participation to those who are athletically gifted to the exclusion of the many, and particularly of those who need it most.
2. Coaching for the sake of winning rather than for the development of the participants, leading to the exploitation of boys and girls.
3. The bringing of sports into the orbit of the gambling interests of the community, local and remote. At the time this is being written the press is full of the accounts of the "throwing" of games or "shaving points" by star basketball players in several universities. The current scandal is the most recent of several instances in other sports.

4. The conducting of the sports program as a separate interest divorced from the learning processes of the school, and often in interference with learning.

5. Illegitimately subsidizing "stars" through means not available to other students of equal ability in other fields.

6. Overemphasis upon competition as a method of personal and group relations.

Leisure time activities other than sports fall roughly under three general types: recreation, amusement, and avocation. Recreation characteristically involves active participation. Amusement, on the other hand, consists in passive participation. An avocation consists in the cultivation of an interest and skill outside of but not inconsistent with one's main interest or occupation.

Recreation as active participation provides opportunities for:

1. Initiative.
2. Creativity.
3. The discovery and development of interests and capacities.
4. Constructive group association.
5. The enrichment of personality through free self-expression.
6. The relief of tension and strain through alternating activity.

Amusement as passive rather than active participation provides opportunity for the enrichment of personality through:

1. Discriminating choice of forms of amusement.
2. The cultivation of appreciation and taste in music, drama, movies, reading, and witnessing sports.
3. The widening of perspectives through deliberately cultivating new receptive experiences.
4. Entering creatively into appreciative experiences, since, as in art, for example, the total esthetic experience is the result of the work of the artist and the reaction of the beholder.

Avocation through the cultivation of correlative interests assumes great importance, especially in view of the lengthening of life expectancy, because:

1. It affords a wider perspective on living.
2. It develops secondary interests and skills that may sometime become useful or necessary.
3. It builds up abiding interests and skills for the years after one's vocational career is ended. With such interests this period of later life may be enriching and rewarding rather than drab and sterile.

As in sports, there are a number of serious dangers to be avoided in recreational activities. Certain forms of recreation and amusement in many communities outside the school are negative in their influence and militate against the constructive efforts of the school. This may be true even within the school community itself. In that event, the school may exert its influence in two directions. On the one hand, it may co-operate with other community agencies, such as the home, the church, and the social agencies, in ridding the community of these negative influences as far as possible and in creating a favorable atmosphere for the development of wholesome ideals. On the other hand, since the environment cannot be changed wholly, it may seek to help children and young people develop a discriminating attitude toward these opportunities, so that their choice of recreational and amusement activities will be selective and constructive.

II

The following are suggestions regarding techniques for helping children and young people develop the value potentials in the areas of sports and recreation.

1. Every individual should have the opportunity to experience some success. Ways may include:

(a) For the person who has a low I. Q. but who is strong physically, provide, if possible, an opportunity to excell in

sports. For example, a good runner or baseball player may
be commended for his excellence in these activities.

(b) Provide individual training for those not skilled.

(c) Provide opportunity for boys and girls with ability to
help those less skilled.

(d) For the boy or girl who is strong mentally but weak
physically, provide opportunities for games that require
skill or strategy but that are not strenuous.

(e) For the person who is weak mentally and physically,
provide giveaway games, opportunity for ringing the bell at
recess or noon where such a system is used, or simple puzzles
and picture cutouts.

(f) Attempt to bring out the timid pupil by permitting
him occasionally to select a game to be played, by having
skilled pupils aid him, or by helping him achieve some success in the group in another way.

(g) Through a wide range of activities, provision may be
made for the interests and abilities of all persons. For example, the poliomyelitis victim may not be able to play
football but may excell at swimming or shuffleboard. One
school provided opportunities for three boys that were not
physically able to participate in athletics to be associated
with the team as scorer, shot-chart keeper, and manager.

(h) Arrange groups for competition on the basis of age,
height, weight or a combination of these items, so that com-
petitors may be of comparable ability.

(i) Use boys and girls as leaders, officials, timers, scorers,
reporters, and scouts.

(j) Extend opportunities by means of interschool programs that include more than the commonly limited range
of activities, the organization of weight, "B," and junior
teams, extended intramural programs, the improvement of
instruction in required physical education, and the utilization
of leadership potentials of all staff members in coaching.

2. Provide opportunities for individual and group creative
experience through:

(a) Participation in the development of rules of safety for
personal and group conduct. This procedure starts in the
nursery in one school.

(b) Participation in planning for picnics, parties, socials.

(c) Participation in the group planning of the required physical education, intramural, and recreational programs.

(d) Offering of the opportunity for instruction and participation in the arts and crafts.

(e) Opportunities for participation in individual- or group-produced pantomimes, skits, or plays.

(f) Opportunities for participation in the activities of the dance program and in the interpretation of symbols, movements, and rhythms.

(g) Opportunities for work with sand in the elementary grades.

(h) The use of mimetic activities in the elementary grades —acting out stories, acting out tasks as washing dishes, and interpreting music by motions.

3. The development of social sensitivity, respect for the opinions of others, a sense of justice, and a sense of responsibility through:

(a) A sharing of ideas in planning and evaluating activities.

(b) Keeping score.

(c) Keeping time.

(d) Participation in parties, hikes, dances, etc.

(e) Provision of the opportunity for the individual to fuse himself with the group through group activity.

(f) Studying the contributions of various races and peoples to sports and recreation.

4. Growth of appreciation of a larger world through:

(a) A study of the play of peoples of all nations.

(b) Participation in folk dances and designing costumes.

(c) A study of the origin of such games as bowling, archery, tennis.

(d) Outdoor activities and hikes: nature study from the standpoint of art, identification and study of wild life and its habits, insight into the complexity and organization of the natural surroundings.

(e) Story hours.

(f) Dramatization.

(g) The making of clay and other models.

All of these may be developed in co-ordination with work in the social studies, art, English, dramatics, science, mathematics, and health.

5. Growth in the discrimination of values through:

(a) Participation in a wide range of activities and an evaluation of them.

(b) As a leader, deciding on the qualities needed by team members.

(c) As a participant, deciding on the qualities of a good leader.

(d) Making of choices of the activity desired when a choice is given.

(e) A recognition of the place various races and peoples have held in the making of records in sports and in the development of games.

(f) The assumption of responsibility for decisions and choices either in participating in or in planning of activities.

6. Appreciation and respect for the body through:

(a) Recognition of the need for a fit body in competition. Competitive athletics and physical education should not be engaged in without a medical checkup. In competitive athletics the checkup should be made at least annually. The student should come to appreciate the results of the examination.

(b) A study of the importance of the various parts of the body in the playing of particular games.

(c) A critical appraisal of good body position or posture in the performance of tasks such as lifting, throwing, running, and pushing.

(d) An appraisal of the physiques of various leaders in sports and the body types that seem to excell in different sports—the lineman, the backs, the basketball center, the sprinter, the distance man.

(e) An understanding of the physiological limits of the body and its quick recovery from fatigue.

(f) Recognition of the effects of illness on condition.

(g) The study of the effects of intemperance in eating, smoking, and drinking upon bodily condition.

7. Growth in the sense of responsibility and accountability through:

(a) Serving as a leader in the choice of games.
(b) Serving as a captain in organized games.
(c) Serving on committees planning parties.
(d) The scouting of opponents.
(e) Assuming responsibility as chairman of a finance committee in the purchase of equipment.
(f) Serving as manager of a team or in intramurals.
(g) Serving as an equipment manager.
(h) Recognition of the responsibility of the follower; of that of leadership.

8. Learning to lose as well as to win graciously through:

(a) Not being boastful in victory.
(b) Failing to give alibis in losing.
(c) Avoiding taking unfair advantage of an opponent.
(d) Withholding degrading remarks about opponents, officials, coaches.
(e) Congratulating opponents in a sincere way following victory or defeat.
(f) Controlling tempers to the best of ability on and off the playing area.
(g) Recognizing and commending good plays of either team.

9. Respect for property through:

(a) Helping in the selection of equipment used in the program of sports and recreation.
(b) Planning the use of budget allotment in the purchase of equipment.
(c) Assisting in the planning and construction of new equipment.
(d) Assisting in the cleaning and storing of equipment.
(e) Assisting in making an inventory of equipment.
(f) Evaluating the importance of well-kept equipment in increased joy of use.

(g) Aiding in the care of courts and playing areas.

(h) Trying out of "loose" and "careful" methods in the use of equipment. Careful handling and responsible use of equipment, a must for the school with little, is desirable in any school in the formation of attitudes.

10. Opportunity for the development of honesty may be provided through:

(a) Making decisions of whether a ball is "in" or "out," "foul" or "fair."

(b) Making decisions as an official, a timer, or a scorer of games.

(c) Evaluation of one's own conduct in reference either to one's true self or to the group.

(d) Being fair to teammates in the matter of training.

(e) Being honest with the coach with reference to training or equipment.

11. A feeling of responsibility to the group and to the community may be developed through:

(a) Recognition of the importance of team play in a team sport or of both members in a dual sport.

(b) Participation as a member of a planning group for recreation outside the school.

(c) A recognition of the effect on community prestige of individual or group conduct on trips or in athletic contests.

III

There are two basic criteria for the construction of a school program for sports and recreation. The first is that the welfare of boys and girls should be the determining factor in the formulation of policies and procedures. The second is that the program of sports and recreation should be integrated with the educational program of the school so that administrators, teachers, and directors or coaches will share a mutual responsibility.

Since much depends upon adequate leadership, major attention should be given to the selection and attitudes of the personnel.

A primary responsibility in this regard rests upon the administration. The administration should assume responsibility for selecting, training, and protecting its leadership in sports and recreation. It should create a higher expectancy in these fields than usually exists. It should require training in this field equal to that required in other fields of teaching. Through some such device as an activities council it should avoid the internal tug of war for pupil time. Through an athletic council or a guiding committee it should by co-operative planning and discussion arrive at a definite policy regarding athletics and recreation. It should encourage better understanding and co-operation between the faculty and the athletic department by faculty-coach participation in the determination of both athletic and academic policies, with a view to establishing approximately the same standards of hours and requirements in both fields.

Worthwhile programs in athletics and recreation cannot be established in a short period of time. This stresses the necessity of developing a philosophy of coaching and giving the coaching profession greater stability. It is unfortunate that in many instances by the time the coach gets enough experience to understand boys he must begin thinking of another position because of the pressures brought to bear upon him.

It is a matter of great importance that training for the constructive use of leisure is needed, and that such training involves all teachers. Encouragement should be given to community-wide planning for recreation leadership. Limited facilities may be augmented by the use of staggered play periods. The development of a recreation program requires long-term planning; some schools are finding a five-year program desirable.

The following suggestions may indicate ways in which the director of athletics may make his program more educational and functional and thereby contribute to the discovery and development of moral and spiritual values.

1. A factual basis for a program:

(a) Secure facts which will provide a defensible basis for the program.

(b) Perform executive acts which will enable the administration to appraise the effect of the acts.

(c) Adopt a policy on a factual basis and do not ask for support on a personal basis.

2. Attitude toward the staff:

(a) Reward and encourage the contribution of ideas and service by the members of the staff; do not accept credit due someone else.

(b) Require all members to be qualified for their positions.

(c) Stress staff selection rather than dismissal as a way of improving the staff.

(d) Delegate authority and responsibility clearly. The duties of large staffs may be understood more definitely by the use of a chart.

(e) Discuss policies and procedures with the staff.

(f) Inform staff members concerning openings in other institutions.

3. Attitude toward students:

(a) Provide student leadership and responsibility; encourage student-staff planning.

(b) Provide the most workable and adequate scheme of student classification possible.

(c) Give recognition for work in sports and recreation, but keep this in line with the general school policy.

(d) Teach skills and games useful in school and later life.

(e) Provide for an extensive program.

(f) Require a medical examination of all participants in physical activities, thus avoiding trouble as well as protecting pupils and director.

4. Attitude toward the public:

(a) Keep the public informed in regard to the educational work you are doing. Though it takes time, it will pay in tenure and understanding.

(b) Keep the department well represented in worthwhile civic organizations.

(c) Operate on a sound financial basis; make a budget and hold to it.

5. Attitude toward the educational system:

(a) See to it that your pursued aims and objectives are in accord with those of education; stand ready to reconsider.

(b) Refrain from embarrassing other faculty members by asking special favors for athletics.

(c) Co-operate rather than contend with other departments.

The realization of the value potentials in sports and recreation will be greatly enhanced by proper teacher-coach relations. The coach will do better to clear his practice schedule with the administration and faculty rather than ask the pupils to secure permission from their teachers. The coach can increase the importance attached by his players and the student body to academic standards by expressing an interest in the work of the pupils, by insisting that athletes arrange for making up work missed, and by taking an intelligent and co-operative attitude toward other areas of school work. The realization on the part of other teachers that for some pupils athletics may make a contribution equal to or greater than other areas of the curriculum may make for a more reasonable point of view than that now taken by some teachers. Emphasis should be upon boys and girls rather than upon subjects or activities.

An activities council will contribute much to a well-rounded and integrated program of sports and recreation. Its membership may include teachers of art, music, dramatics, the athletic coach, the athletic director, and representatives of the student body. Its functions are to survey the athletic and recreational interests and needs of the school community, to provide adequate opportunities for sports and recreation, to build a well-rounded program, to arrange a calendar of activities, and to establish general policies.

The athletic council gives continuity, strength, and guidance to the athletic program. It should determine policies; have on its membership the superintendent, principal, athletic director, coaches of the several sports, supervisors of physical education, and the financial manager or treasurer; provide for making awards on a merit basis; determine the number of games to be played in each sport; determine the number of participants in each sport; provide adequate equipment; provide a trainer who is an expert in first aid; provide insurance; provide physical examinations; allocate authority of the staff; finance the program; co-ordinate the program with that of other departments; and provide administration and supervision of the program.

CHAPTER FOURTEEN

Techniques of Synthesis:
Symbolic Expression

THE TECHNIQUES of analysis are concerned with the breaking down of the school experience into specific situations in order to locate the value potentials inherent in them. The learning process, especially as related to living, requires that these disparate learnings shall be brought together into functioning wholes in the form of generalized meanings, convictions, and ideals, and, at the highest level through revaluation, into a philosophy of life. After analysis should come synthesis. This is primarily the function of symbols, which are for the most part art forms. Art, like religion, is a comprehending experience in which life is seen, felt, and appreciated in wholes.

I

A symbol is a formalized overt expression under varying forms of an organized system of meanings and values.

The source of all symbols of whatever form is the meanings and values that are generated in personal and social experience. Like personality, they are predominantly social products.

There are many types of symbols. One of them takes the form of gesture. Gesture, accompanied by inarticulate sounds, was the earliest means of communication among primitives. In its most sophisticated form it is used by modern man in the drama and the dance, as well as in religious liturgy. Another type takes the form of meaningful ob-

jects, such as the churinga and the totem pole among primitives, and the fraternity pin, the engagement ring, the flag,
the swastika, the hammer and sickle, the Star of David, the
cross, and the insignia of military rank. Language is one of
the most important forms of symbols, as in the spoken or
written word, the scientific formula, creeds, mottoes, and
slogans, such as "Remember the Maine!" "Blood and Soil,"
"The New Deal," "America First." Among the more elaborate forms are ceremonials, as in ground-breaking, dedications, laying of cornerstones, installations, ordinations, and
the celebration of the Eucharist. So also are celebrations,
such as Thanksgiving, Christmas, founders' day, anniver-
saries, festivals, and Armistice Day.

Symbols operate on different psychological levels. In some
instances they function on the unconscious and irrational
level, as in response to the cry of "Fire!" in a crowded theater.
At other times they act on the semiconscious level, with a
minimum of intellectual content, as in response to the party
or national emblem. But at the highest level they perform
with a maximum of intellectual content, as in the case of
highly abstract philosophical and scientific discourse and in
the use of mathematical and scientific formulas, as in
$MC^2 = E$, the formula for atomic energy.

Roughly, it may be said that the function of symbols in
relation to experience is fivefold. First, the symbol is the
means of making articulate and explicit a meaning or value
that has arisen out of experience. Second, as a condensed
stimulus, the symbol is a means of recalling and reawakening
the original response to a meaning or value after the original
situation that gave rise to the meaning or value is past. Thus,
what otherwise might be ephemeral and fugitive is rendered
permanent and is absorbed into the social system of meanings and values. Third, symbols are means of communication. They are the most effective media for sharing meanings
and values among contemporaries within and beyond the

immediate social group, and for transmitting meanings and values from one generation to another over long periods of time, thus making possible "the great conversation." In this way symbols are enriched and kept alive. Fourth, symbols are a means of social control. At the unconscious and unintentional level, symbols approved by the group exert a psychological constraint upon the individual. On the conscious and intentional level, the symbol is deliberately used to secure conformity, as in the use of the creed to establish a standard of orthodoxy in religion, Hitler's lavish use of the swastika and pageantry in the Sportsplatz, and the Kremlin's unprecedented use of propaganda. So also in a constructive and creative way symbols may be used to give a structure of meanings and values in a community of self-realizing persons. Fifth, symbols, chiefly as art forms, gather together meanings and values in many specific situations into generalized meanings and values. Thus, the word "honesty" expresses a generalized attitude and way of behaving. Drama sets forth in imaginative form certain points of view and reflections on life, as in the case of "Thanksgiving 2000 A.D.," analyzed in Chapter IX. "The Blue Vase," analyzed in the same chapter, gathers up into an art object a complex of appreciations of beauty. Symbols are comprehensive in their nature and integrate many fragmentary experiences by viewing them as wholes.

It is clear, therefore, that symbolic expression is a fundamental and indispensable step in the discovery and development of moral and spiritual values. Until they are definitely identified and clearly explicated they are apt to remain vague, amorphous, and elusive. Notwithstanding what has been said about starting with traits or virtues as the beginning point in a program for developing moral and spiritual values, the necessity of arriving at traits or virtues that are convincingly valid and compellingly real is even more important. This is the function of symbols which, while not neglectful of verbal labels or even slogans, lay hold upon the rich and inexhaustible, and often all but neglected, resources of poetry, music, painting, the plastic arts, and drama not only to identify these values, but to give them depth of meaning and to render them appealing.

On the other hand, there are certain dangers in the use of symbols. The tendency of symbols is to become stereotyped and thus to become inflexible and resistant to enrichment and growth in meaning through new experience. There is also a tendency for the symbol to be substituted for the value it symbolizes, so that the present response is to the symbol and not to the reality which it represents. This, in the view of Professor H. N. Wieman (*The Source of Human Good*), is a major source of evil in human experience. The symbol may be used, deliberately or unintentionally, to cultivate false loyalties, as in the case of sectarianism versus a universal outlook in religion, or nationalism versus an inclusive human society of justice and peace. Symbols may be used inaccurately, so that the meaning does not correspond to reality, as in the dichotomy between "sacred" and "secular," or the "material" and the "spiritual," as discussed earlier in this book. There is also danger of overcelebrating in a crowded school schedule.

If symbols are to be meaningful and real, they must grow out of the experience of the school community. Teachers, administrators, and students must be sensitive to meanings and values and to their emergence in the school experience. They must then together have enough imagination, resourcefulness, and creativity to create suitable expression for them through literary forms, music, the plastic arts, drama, painting, and the dance. In this the aim should be not so much at artistic perfection as expressiveness, though the highest practicable degree of excellence and taste should be striven for. And for this purpose there already exists a vast fund of resource material in art forms that have arisen out of the experience of the past and are relevant to current experience.

II

There are many resources, often overlooked, for the discovery and use of symbols in commonplace experiences, such as trips to historic sites and institutions, exhibits, and programs. Out of a wealth of illustrations collected by the group on symbolic expression, a few are selected as indicating what imaginative and resourceful teachers may do in their own situations.

A Glee Club Visits Duncan Tavern. The Glee Club received an invitation to give the Christmas program for the Delta Kappa Gamma at Duncan Tavern.

In preparation for the program a study was made of carols, customs, traditions, and peoples of other lands. The girls selected a program they thought symbolic of some of our more familiar Christmas customs which have been borrowed from other nations through the ages.

After the program they were taken through the building and given first the history of the building and then the background of many of its beautiful furnishings and displays representative of the culture of our forefathers.

Many of the girls wanted to return and get a better look at some particular thing. Others were interested in the different periods of history shown there.

A Journey to Lexington for the 1950 All-State Chorus. This activity each year is significant because it requires a high degree of preparation, concentration, and a strong sense of group responsibility.

This incident re-emphasizes the fact that spiritual values endure after material benefits are gone.

The leader of the chorus was a personable young man from a big-name radio program. He included in his program "Give Me Your Tired, Your Poor," by Irving Berlin, from the musical show, "Miss Liberty." The words of this song were copied from the inscription on the Statue of Liberty, taken from the sonnet, "The New Colossus," by Emma Lazarus:

> Not like the brazen giant of Greek fame,
> With conquering limbs astride from land to land;

Here at our sea-washed, sunset gates shall stand
A mighty woman with a torch, whose flame
Is the imprisoned lightning, and her name
Mother of Exiles. From her beacon hand
Glows world-wide welcome; her mild eyes command
The air-bridged harbor that twin cities frame.
"Keep, ancient lands, your storied pomp!" cries she
With silent lips. "Give me your tired, your poor,
Your huddled masses yearning to breathe free,
The wretched refuse of your teeming shore.
Send these, the homeless, tempest-tossed, to me.
I lift my lamp beside the golden door!"

When this song was mentioned the whole chorus applaud-
ed wildly. They begged for it during practice sessions and
sang it on the program as though they were inspired and had
seen a new light.

What was that light? Perhaps kindness, generosity, faith,
loyalty, and principles of eternal truth, but certainly a vision
of the American dream.

A Mathematics Class. In the seventh-grade arithmetic
class the children study figures and solids. In order that
the children may have a more meaningful understanding of
their shape and form, recognize them easily, and see that
they have use in everyday living, a trip around the school
and out into the community provides pleasure and firsthand
experiences. These figures and solids can be found within
the symbols of our nation's foundation—church, home, and
school—and they make a triangle on which our very existence
rests.

Before thinking of church, home, and school, there are
symbols to be found in nature—God's handiwork. The tree
trunks are cylinders; branches and leaves silhouetted against
the sky look like triangles—in fact they are really in the
shape of a cone. The sun and moon look like circles, but
they are thought of as spheres.

The churches, schools, and houses in which we live have
examples of these figures and solids. These are man-made
as a result of his efforts to make things strong and beautiful
as well as useful. The beauty of the circle and the simplicity
of the rectangle can be pointed out in various forms of archi-

tecture. In addition, students can be shown the strength of the arch—an example that can be found in the nature of the rainbow.

Children should look in the houses in which they live to find triangles in the gables, rectangles in the windows and doors, cylinders in the columns. Inside the house they discover that the rooms are rectangular solids and the arches are part of a curve. Even some pieces of furniture are true solids.

Churches, schools, and other public buildings are rich in these forms, though they are used in a much more elaborate manner. The spire of the church, the stained glass windows, the furnishing back of the altar, the doorway into the sanctuary, designs on walls and over doorways—all reveal much of what is in the mind of man. So many of these point upward as a symbol of the higher values in life.

In all these experiences of seeing what God has given us and what man has done to glorify His gifts, either in the simple setting of a small house or the vastness of public buildings, the child is helped to develop an appreciation of the things about him.

An Indian Program. After a study on Indians, the second graders wanted to give a program. During the study the music teacher had been helpful and had taught several little songs. The children decided that songs, dances, stories, and poems could be used. Two little children, a boy and a girl, wrote short papers on "How the Indians Get Food," and "How the Indians Make Their Clothes." These children wore Indian outfits and read their papers. Twelve children gave an Indian dance. Two poems and one story were on the program. The height of the program was the song, "Ten Little Indian Boys." Ten little boys, graduated in height, sang and acted out the song. They were dressed in costume, complete with headdress and war paint.

A Fifth-Grade Music Program. The story of America is written in music. Its songs are symbols of its unfolding life from the pioneer wilderness days to the present.

Music was part of Indian life before the coming of the white man. It began with the crooning of lullabies by the

Indian mother to the babe swung in his cradle on her back. It throbbed in the beats of the tom-tom that called the Indian to the warpath. "Indian Planting."

Then came the Pilgrims to the new land seeking religious liberty. They were a stern and hardy people, making their living from a reluctant New England soil. They had little time for music or pleasure. But their hymns reflected the religious belief of their daily lives. Today we pay homage to their courage and faith, though through a hymn of Catholic origin. "Faith of Our Fathers."

Gayer notes were heard in the southern colonies. Here happy maidens and their swains danced the Virginia reel. "Clar the Kitchen."

In Old Virginia in 1774 on a warm spring evening hundreds of candles were lighted in the stately parlor. Carriages from plantation homes arrived bringing gentlemen and ladies for an evening of music and dancing. A group of musicians played the minuet. "Don Juan Minuet."

Music came to New York and Pennsylvania with the happy, fun-loving Dutch settlers. It spread through the coastal colonies as they grew in numbers. Then one day the voices of the thirteen original colonies rose together in one lively song breathing defiance to the mother country. A rousing marching song of Revolutionary times is still a favorite of Americans everywhere. "Yankee Doodle."

The Revolutionary War brought freedom to the colonies, but a growing America was again involved in conflict with the British—this time for the freedom of the seas. After a long night of anxious waiting, Francis Scott Key, a prisoner on a British warship, saw the stars and stripes still waving, and our National Anthem was born. "The Star-Spangled Banner."

With the growing of cotton in the South and the coming of the Negroes, a new type of music enriched the musical heritage of America, with new tempo, new rhythm. The Negro spirituals are favorites all over America. "Steal Away."

Differences between the North and the South over slavery and state's rights involved the nation in Civil War. Again music went to war in Julia Ward Howe's "Battle Hymn of the Republic."

Subsequent to the assassination of Abraham Lincoln and the rebuilding of the nation, tides of immigration from Europe brought many people with many diverse cultural heritages to America. Symbolic of the culture heritage they brought were their songs. Typical of these was "The Blue Bells of Scotland."

In 1914 America became involved in World War I which was productive of many martial songs. Typical of the songs used was "When Johnny Comes Marching Home," from Civil War days.

The Second World War was not so prolific in songs, but it revived many martial songs already familiar and added some new ones. Among these were "The Marine Hymn," "The Caisson Song," and "The Air Force Song."

And now America, together with the other free peoples of the world, is desperately trying to find a way by which a just and lasting peace may be established for all men. Something of this wistful yearning is expressed in "God Bless America."

III

As we turn from the informal sources of symbols in the everyday experiences of the school community, we find an inexhaustible source of symbolic expression in the more formal and elaborate forms of ceremonials and celebrations.

A mere listing of the occasions for celebration and ceremonials is sufficient to suggest their endless possibilities. Among them are historical events, such as Armistice Day, Pearl Harbor Day, Flag Day, Memorial Day, Independence Day, and current noteworthy events. Among the stated holidays and observances are Halloween, Labor Day, Thanksgiving, Christmas, New Year's Day, Valentine Day, St. Patrick's Day, Mother's Day, Father's Day, Arbor Day, and Music Week. Among local school events are such items as exhibitions, homecomings, class days, victory in athletic contests, commencements, opening of school, conclusions of units of study, dedications of buildings, cornerstone layings, ground-breakings, recognition awards, and founders' day observances. The birthdays of great personalities are fruit-ful occasions of celebrations, such as those of Washington, Lincoln, Roosevelt, Einstein, Helen Keller, Bell, Wright brothers, Clay, Lee, Florence Nightingale, Pasteur, Bach, Beethoven, Newton, and famous local historic persons.

Celebrations and ceremonies, when rightly used, present unusual opportunities for the stressing of moral and spiritual values in which they are inherently rich. The greatest sig-nificance will be attained, however, if the pupils themselves, with the help of teachers, become conscious of the values in-volved and choose or create an appropriate symbolic ex-pression. Unless the pupils share in the effort, there is danger that the celebration or ceremonial will become mere-ly a "program," imposed upon them from the outside and with meager significance to the pupil. Always it should be remembered that the significance of the symbol derives from its direct relation to the experience symbolized, whether it is taken from the cumulative treasury of inherited symbols or is created *de novo*. It may be useful here again to em-phasize the caution against overcelebration, though most schools are likely to err in the direction of not making enough of the resources of celebrations and ceremonies.

Space permits the selection of only a few illustrations of the more formal forms of symbolic expression. These will suffice to indicate, however, what imaginative and resourceful teachers may do with their pupils in creating ceremonials or celebrations suitable to their own situations.

The following is a dramatic presentation worked out by one teacher with her pupils to symbolize the values of brotherhood, open-mindedness, and international co-opera-tion, with deep religious implications:

Education for the Atomic Age

Scene 1

A posed picture suggesting education. Two boys bending over a microscope and two boys in caps and gowns, one

handing a diploma to the other. A voice from the side reads
the sonnet, "Commencement Address," by Jacob C. Solovay:

Cling fast to learning, you who bid farewell,
With ribboned scroll clutched tightly in your hand,
Proud in your moment's wonder as you stand
Between two worlds like one caught in a spell.
Wisdom is living, yes, but where you live
Determines wisdom too, and printed words
Have given man the wings of eager birds,
To ride the peaks which only mountains give.
Here at the first great Rubicon you quail,
Between the sheltered past and what will be,
With backward glances and uneasy looks.
Have courage, for without it you will fail;
Have justice, it will help to make you free;
And burn your bridges, but don't burn your books.

(Curtain)

Scene II (a schoolroom)

The teacher is pointing to the theme which is printed on
the blackboard with the formula $MC^2 = E$ and the atomic
sign. A boy is looking on. Five or six charts of leading nations (America, England, Russia, France, and Japan) are
on display. The charts contain information such as population, area, natural resources, food production, power, etc.
The teacher goes from one to the other, explaining the
charts. At this point Uncle Sam enters as a visitor and perhaps as a philosopher.

Teacher: I see we have a visitor. Do come in.

Uncle Sam: Oh! I'm sorry. I didn't mean to disturb you.
Go right ahead.

Teacher: I am now explaining our relations to other
leading nations.

Uncle Sam: Very good (looking at pupil) . You are now
getting many different experiences here at school. This
makes for a great nation.

Pupil: How does that come about?

Uncle Sam: Because you will know better how to adjust
yourself to life and new conditions. You should be self-
directed, with an open, inquiring mind, and yet be dependent on others.

Pupil: I have learned in school how to depend on myself.

Uncle Sam: That is good, but one should go further than that. I was thinking today as we looked at these posters, how is it possible to achieve a real unity among the United Nations? Have you any ideas?

Pupil: Surely, by common political action, of course.

Uncle Sam: Do you think there could be such common action among nations unless they held certain ideas in common?

Pupil: No.

Uncle Sam: Then common ideas are necessary for common action. I assume that we are talking about ideas that are both moral and spiritual.

Pupil: Yes, good ideas and good action. Is the U.N. a step toward United Civilization?

Uncle Sam: I think so. The ideas of the various civilizations would be the common basis of the United Nations.

Pupil: Who is helping them to pool their ideas?

Uncle Sam: UNESCO is interested in being their teacher. UNESCO is telling them why they should live together in mutual understanding.

Pupil: UNESCO is preaching peace? Peace and a treaty?

Uncle Sam: UNESCO has in mind a better peace, a peace not signed with blood on a battlefield, but signed with truth, moral and spiritual virtue, in the hearts and lives of men.

Pupil: You know, I have been thinking about the United States and Russia, who fought side by side against a common foe. They are now opposed to each other. Suppose they turned to war against each other?

Uncle Sam: The winner would be forced to set up a universal military state.

Pupil: What if neither won?

Uncle Sam: The result would be the same, for another power would step in and our civilization would perish.

Pupil: Not if we hang on to the atomic bomb.

Uncle Sam: Why has everyone become so narrowed and bewitched by the black and secret magic of the atomic bomb?

Pupil: Well, because of the way the Atomic Commission is handling the situation. Our secret is leaking out.

Uncle Sam: Our nation's problems are great. Their very size leads some men to refuse to face them, and instead of solving them by work, by hard and clear critical thinking, they are throwing themselves into the protective arms of a mysterious bomb.

Pupil: If we are not careless and watch our secret, all will be safe.

Uncle Sam: Yes, (sorrowfully) I am getting the idea that some people think it is as simple as that. Just tie our hopes and our problems in one package, a parcel guarded by a watchman.

Pupil: Oh, I see what you mean, something like a B movie.

Uncle Sam: Exactly, can't you see us? We are digging in an atomic dump for a bottle called "National Destiny."

Pupil: You mean that if we pin all our hopes of safety on the bomb we are alone; we are locked in a world in which there is no safety whatever.

Uncle Sam: Yes, there can be no air or sunlight, no open windows or unlocked doors.

Pupil: Oh, I'm beginning to see, "no locked doors, no iron curtain."

Uncle Sam: You are on the right track. This is still a world of coherent historical process. Our safety lies in our faith in each other; if we lose that, we will be weak regardless of what we develop or own. Only youth with an open mind will learn new ways to meet this atomic age.

A mixed quartet or other small ensemble closes the program with the singing of the "Prayer Universal," by Lona Hagstrom, set to music by Charles W. Cadman:

> O great Creator of mankind,
> Grant us Thy wisdom now, we pray
> With justice and discerning truth
> To solve the problems of our day.
> O teach Thy children gathered here,
> Whate'er their creed or race or birth,
> One language understood by love
> And glorified by human worth.
> O heal the wounds past wars have made;
> Blot out old grievances and blot out old hates,
> And bind us with Thy Father love
> Into one vast United States.

(Curtain)

The following shows how a fifth grade worked out with the teacher's help a Columbus Day program:

The fifth-grade children gave a program on Columbus Day. Songs, poems, and one short story were presented. As a narrator gave a simple history of America from the discovery down to the present time, a series of scenes depicting highlights of certain periods were presented in pantomime by several different groups of children. All the groups wore costumes and these made a colorful program. The minuet, danced by twelve children, was a delightful scene. All the children in the fifth grade had a part in this program.

Retrospect and Prospect

THIS ACCOUNT of an experimental program for the discovery and development of moral and spiritual values in education may well conclude with an interpretative retrospect on its progress thus far and a forward look into its potential future.

I

The changing problem of moral and spiritual values in American education has been viewed in relation to the dynamic changes in American culture. The contemporary situation demands a new approach and a new solution. In the light of the present world situation, it begins to appear that perhaps the most pressing task that confronts our generation, next to achieving a just and lasting peace, is the restoration of a proper balance between science, technology, and industrial development on the one hand, and the value content in our culture on the other. This responsibility rests directly upon the school, along with other institutions—perhaps more so. An unprecedented urgency in this undertaking arises out of the present world conflict in which democracy as a way of life is placed in jeopardy by the ruthless pressures of the totalitarian slave state. When viewed in this historical and social context, a program of moral and spiritual values in education ceases to be just another development in educational theory and practice and takes on immense cultural dimensions.

II

Viewed in retrospect, the program of moral and spiritual values interpreted in this volume has been the outgrowth of the deep concern of the citizens of one commonwealth over the neglect of moral and spiritual values in contemporary American education and an attempt to do something about it.

From the beginning it has been a co-operative movement, jointly sponsored by the University of Kentucky, the University of Louisville, Murray State College, Western State College, Eastern State College, and Morehead State College. The nontax-supported colleges have been represented at the advisory level on the Advisory Committee. It has recognized the strict separation of church and state. It is neither in competition with or a substitute for the work of the churches in the field of religious education. It has assumed that functional moral and spiritual values, unencumbered with theological or ecclesiastical interpretations, may be experienced by pupils from the earliest age as inherent in the life process. On the other hand, such division of function and responsibility in no way inhibits the fullest understanding and co-operation of the school and the churches in a shared responsibility for the development of the child and youth life of the total community. It has assumed that moral and spiritual values are autonomous and inhere in the essential nature of the school community and the educative process. Therefore the formula: "the discovery and development of moral and spiritual values." The movement has also stressed the autonomous nature of motivation when these values are functionally related to the actual experience of growing persons through ego-involvement in end-seeking activity, thus insuring attitudes and intentions that will carry beyond verbalization to action.

The more the movement has found itself, the more definitely it has become a movement of emphasis. The better teachers and the better schools have all along been concerned with moral and spiritual values. But the emphasis for the most part has been sporadic, personal, and incidental. No new courses or content is needed. What is needed is that the emphasis upon moral and spiritual values be explicitly included in the objectives of the school and that administrators, teachers, and pupils become sensitive to the emergence of these values as they arise in the school community, the curriculum, counseling, sports and recreation, and every other activity of the school.

The movement has sought to provide a rational basis for its program in a well-considered formulation of a philosophy in keeping with modern trends in educational theory and practice. With the conviction arising out of this philosophy that thinking and practice should not be divorced, the movement has from the beginning been experimental. It has been based upon the experience of school administrators and teachers in actual school situations. The pilot experimental schools were set up for the purpose of discovering and formulating procedures and for testing them in teaching situations. Thus far the movement has avoided stereotypes, seeking new insights, new leads, and new directions for the future. This seems to be one of the most important characteristics of the program.

It has throughout been a democratic movement. Superintendents, principals, and teachers have together worked out their procedures through inquiry, discussion, planning, execution, and judging. In this process they have discovered that differences are resources rather than liabilities and that one's experience is extended and enriched by trying to understand another's point of view and why he holds it. By such meeting of minds in a shared quest, tolerance, which is a negative concept, has given way to creative and constructive appreciation. Thus, working together in the workshops and experimental schools, superintendents, principals, and teachers have themselves entered into the *experience* of moral and spiritual valus. Working at this level carries the educative process beyond a merely formal professional activity into something that is releasing, inspiring, and creative. Teachers have repeatedly said that the year of experimentation has been the most satisfying of their professional careers. One teacher in particular has spoken of her entire outlook on life having been changed. Students have spontaneously offered similar comments.

III

The movement has passed through its first phase of formulation and initial experimentation. It now enters upon its second phase of refinement, correction, and confirmation in a wider range of school experience as well as of extension. Several important developments have marked the beginning of the second phase of development. One is the incorporation of the results of the workshops and experimentation into the Kentucky Department of Education's *Curriculum Guide* for the elementary and secondary schools of the state. The second has been the introduction during the summer of 1951 of workshops or courses into the tax-supported teacher-education institutions of the state for teachers in service and teachers in preparation. The tax-supported colleges of education in the state have, with the beginning of 1951, taken responsibility for the spread of the movement in the regions of the state served by each of the respective colleges. Each college has financed its own program, and is making plans for follow-up work during the school year with the teachers, principals, and superintendents who participated in the 1951 summer school seminars or workshops. The third has been through the release by the Lincoln Foundation of half the time of its Director J. Mansir Tydings, and a generous grant from the Lily Endowment, to make possible field direction of the program throughout the commonwealth. Dr. William H. Kilpatrick served as consultant to several of the workshops.

As illustrative of numerous further developments in the area of procedures, three may be mentioned. First, it is clear that one of the great needs of the immediate future is the development of scientific methods for measuring changing attitudes and conduct, a step not feasible within the limits of the first two workshops or the initial courses in teacher-education institutions. Much preliminary work has been done in this field by the Character Education Inquiry and such techniques for measuring attitudes as those developed by the Thurstone-Chave studies. This undertaking is as difficult as it is necessary in order to validate detailed aspects of basic theory and the procedures employed. There may be considerable question about the adequacy of existing measurement techniques in the field of growth in the appreciation and realization of moral and spiritual values and the way in which they affect personal and group behavior. Such tests as are here proposed will need to measure the dynamics of the growth of the whole person and not merely isolated and static traits. Useful as the conventional statistical procedures may be for dealing with norms and deviations in mass data, they leave much to be desired in the measurement of growth in relation to dynamic behavior patterns, especially in the areas of intentions and motives. Perhaps the direction in which the needed measurement of moral and spiritual values may lie will be in the refined use of individual case and group histories. Teacher-education institutions with their technically trained staffs have an unusual opportunity and responsibility in this area.

Second, there is need for the development of what under the limitations of the first two workshops have of necessity been anecdotal accounts of cases into fully elaborated case histories which will include such items as a detailed description of the situation in which the behavior arose; a careful analysis of the antecedent factors of heredity, temperament, health; social status, education, and all knowable conditioning factors; a detailed description of the procedure in dealing with the situation; and the recoverable consequents of the event. Valuable as would be the raw data resulting from the collection of such a body of case material, its chief value would lie in the working out and validation of generalized techniques of guidance for the use of administrators, teachers, and pupils in understanding, predicting, and controlling the responses of growing persons of varied backgrounds, capacities, and interests to the situations that life in and beyond the school presents to them. One fundamentally important aspect of such a generalized procedure would be that in dealing with individual differences there can be no stereotyped procedure, but, within a generalized pattern, as much flexibility and variation as the unique individual experience may demand.

Third, a way needs to be found for educatively relating the child or youth as a whole person to the total range of his varied and often conflicting experiences in interacting with different phases of his natural, social, cultural, and cosmic world. As yet the child or youth is not envisioned by many, if not most, teachers and parents as a total dynamic self, and few, if any, ways have been discovered for knitting his disparate experiences into a cumulative and consistent whole. The core curriculum of some elementary and secondary schools is a step in this direction.

IV

In any case, the discovery and development of moral and spiritual values in education confronts the public school with a challenge that is at once urgent and difficult—the most urgent and difficult in the whole field of education. If in the past the school has on the whole reflected and confirmed the existing cultural pattern, the time has come for it to assume the role of creative leadership in helping society to examine and reappraise the ends it seeks and the means by which it would achieve them. The school as the most authentic interpreter of American culture must accept the responsibility of leadership in helping to redress the existing imbalance between the brilliant advances in science, technology, and production on the one hand, and esthetic, moral, spiritual, and social values on the other. This is no simple or easy task to be accomplished by conventional procedures. It is a colossal undertaking, demanding our utmost resources of intelligence, imagination, and creativity.

While it would be a false and cruel indictment to say that the schools have been indifferent to moral and spiritual values, the experience of the experimental schools would indicate that this emphasis in any systematic and planned form that erects moral and spiritual values to a position of the primary objective of the school program is definitely something new in recent American education. The fact that the Educational Policies Commission made this the high priority concern for 1950 may indicate that one of the next most important developments in American education may be the reinstatement of the value content in our educational program.

As Mrs. Margaret Hicks Williams, Director of the British Commonwealth and Northern European Section, Public Affairs Overseas Program, Department of State, Washington, D.C., pointed out in her address at the final session of the second workshop, those who are working in this field of values are working on a new American frontier:

"Inspired democracy must become again the passion of our personal living and the framework of our political planning. The choice is between materialistic motives or moral standards. On this choice depends the future of mankind.

"Every man faces this choice. Every man can shape the future by placing himself under the government of God and by living absolute moral standards. As I am, so is my nation, and this is why what you are doing at the University of Kentucky is of such great significance.

"Americans pride themselves on being pioneers.

"A new type of pioneering must be undertaken today—where we push the frontiers of democracy across the ranges of men's minds, across the wastelands of men's hearts, across the dangerous valleys of men's fears. In a world where aggressive ideologies are shaping the future, we must pioneer our own. And not tomorrow, but today.

"We must mobilize morally or perish."

Thus, those who are working in this area in the various experimental programs that are under way in the nation are living and working on the growing edge of Western culture and of the dynamic experiment in democracy bequeathed to us by the Founding Fathers, with such resources of inventiveness, imagination, and values as we possess. Of one thing we may be assured: in working at the level of values we are working at the highest level of education and, in the largest dimensions of our task, at the growing edge of that *process* which Whitehead would have us understand *is reality,* where the forces of the universe are at work continually creating a new and, we hope, a still better world for ourselves and for all mankind.

A Selected Bibliography

PART ONE

American Council on Education. *The Relation of Religion to Public Education*. Washington, D.C.: American Council on Education, 1947.

Arrowood, C. F. *Thomas Jefferson and Education in a Republic*. New York: McGraw-Hill Book Co., Inc., 1930.

Beard, Charles A. *The Unique Function of Education in a Democracy*. Washington, D.C.: Educational Policies Commission, 1937.

Bower, W. C. *Church and State in Education*. Chicago: University of Chicago Press, 1944.

Bower, W. C. and Hayward, P. R. *Protestantism Faces Its Educational Task Together*. Appleton, Wisc.: C. C. Nelson, 1949.

Brown, S. W. *The Secularization of American Education*. New York: Bureau of Publications, Teachers College, Columbia University, 1912.

Brown, W. A. *Church and State in Contemporary America*. New York: Charles Scribner's Sons, 1936.

Character Education. Washington, D.C.: Department of Superintendence, National Education Association, 1932.

Cubberley, E. P. *Public Education in the United States*. Boston: Houghton Mifflin Co., 1919.

Davis, M. D. *Weekday Classes in Religious Education on Released Time for Public School Pupils*. Washington, D.C.: U.S. Office of Education, 1941.

Deferrari, Roy J. *Essays on Catholic Education in the United States*. Washington, D.C.: Catholic University of America Press, 1942.

——————. *Vital Problems of Catholic Education in the United States*. Washington, D.C.: Catholic University of America Press, 1939.

Educational Policies Commission. *Moral and Spiritual Values in the Public Schools*. Washington, D.C.: National Education Association, 1950.

The Essential Place of Religion in Education. Ann Arbor: National Education Association, 1916.

Henderson, J. C. *Thomas Jefferson's Views on Education.* New York: Putnam, 1890.

Hinsdale, B. A. *Horace Mann and the Common School Revival in the United States.* New York: Charles Scribner's Sons, 1898.

Jackson, J. C. and Malmberg, C. F. *Religious Education and the State.* New York: Doubleday, Doran & Co., 1928.

Mann, Horace. *The Common School Controversy.* Boston: J. N. Bradley & Co., 1844.

Moehlman, C. H. *The American Constitution and Religion.* Berne, Ind.: privately published, 1938.

New York: Ginn & Co., 1936.

Rugg, Harold. *American Life and the School Curriculum.*

——————— (ed.) *Democracy and the Curriculum.* New York: Appleton-Century Co., 1939.

Smith, H. L. *Character Development through Moral and Religious Education in the Public Schools of the United States.* Bloomington, Ind.: University of Indiana Press, 1937.

Smith, S. M. *The Relation of the State to Religious Education.* Syracuse, N. Y.: Syracuse University Press, 1926.

The State and Sectarian Education. Washington, D.C.: Research Bulletin, Vol. XXIV, No. 1, Research Division, National Education Association, 1946.

Van Dusen, H. P. and others. *Church and State in the Modern World.* New York: Harper and Bros., 1937.

White House Conference on Children in a Democracy: Final Report. Washington, D.C.: Department of Labor, 1940.

PART TWO

Adler, Alfred. *Understanding Human Nature.* New York: Greenburg & Co., 1946.

Allport, F. H. *Social Psychology.* Boston: Houghton Mifflin, 1924.

Allport, Gordon. *The Nature of Personality.* Cambridge, Mass.: Addison-Wesley Press, 1950.

Bernard, L. L. *Introduction to Social Psychology.* New York: Henry Holt Co., 1936.

Bibliography

Bower, W. C. *Character through Creative Experience.* Chicago: University of Chicago Press, 1930.

——————. *The Curriculum of Religious Education.* New York: Charles Scribner's Sons, 1925.

——————. *Religion and the Good Life.* New York: Abingdon, 1933.

Burnham, W. H. *The Wholesome Personality.* New York: Appleton, 1932.

Charters, W. W. *The Teaching of Ideals.* New York: Macmillan, 1933.

Chave, E. J. *A Functional Approach to Religious Education.* Chicago: University of Chicago Press, 1947.

——————. *Personality Development in Children.* Chicago: University of Chicago Press, 1937.

Coe, G. A. *Motives of Men.* New York: Charles Scribner's Sons, 1928.

Dennison, J. H. *The Enlargement of Personality.* New York: Charles Scribner's Sons, 1930.

Dewey, John. *Creative Intelligence.* New York: Holt, 1917.

——————. *Democracy and Education.* New York: Macmillan, 1916.

——————. *How We Think.* Boston: D. C. Heath, 1910.

——————. *Human Nature and Conduct.* New York: Carlton House, 1922.

——————. *Interest and Effort.* Boston: Houghton Mifflin, 1913.

——————. *Moral Principles in Education.* Boston: Houghton Mifflin, 1909.

Follett, M. P. *Creative Experience.* New York: Longmans, Green & Co., 1924.

Germane, C. E. and Germane, E. G. *Character Education.* New York: Silver Burdette, 1929.

Hart, J. K. *A Social Interpretation of Education.* New York: Henry Holt & Co., 1929.

Hartshorne, Hugh, *Character in Human Relations.* New York: Charles Scribner's Sons, 1932.

Hartshorne, Hugh and May, Mark. *Studies in Deceit.* New York: Macmillan, 1928.

——————. *Studies in Service and Self-Control.* New York: Macmillan, 1929.

190 Bibliography

Hartshorne, H., May, M., and Shuttleworth, F. K. *Studies in the Organization of Character.* New York: Macmillan, 1930.

Heaton, K. L. *Character Emphasis in Education.* Chicago: University of Chicago Press, 1933.

Holt, E. B. *The Freudian Wish.* New York: Henry Holt & Co., 1915.

Jung, C. G. *Modern Man in Search of a Soul.* New York: Harcourt, Brace & Co., 1933.

Kilpatrick, W. H. *Foundations of Method.* New York: Macmillan, 1925.

————. *Philosophy of Education.* New York: Macmillan, 1951.

————. *Sourcebook in the Philosophy of Education.* New York: Macmillan, 1934.

Mead, G. H. *Mind, Self, and Society.* Chicago: University of Chicago Press, 1934.

————. *The Philosophy of the Act.* Chicago: University of Chicago Press, 1938.

Mearns, Hughes. *Creative Youth.* Garden City: Doubleday Page, 1926.

Meland, B. E. *America's Spiritual Culture.* New York: Harpers, 1948.

Morgan, J. J. B. *The Psychology of Abnormal People.* New York: Longmans, Green & Co., 1928.

Plant, J. S. *Personality and the Culture Pattern.* New York: Commonwealth Fund, 1937.

Roback, A. A. *The Psychology of Character.* New York: Harcourt, Brace & Co., 1927.

Shaw, Clifford. *Delinquency Areas.* Chicago: University of Chicago Press, 1929.

Symonds, P. *Diagnosing Personality and Conduct.* New York: Century, 1931.

Tead, Ordway. *Education for Character: A Neglected Objective.* New Haven: Hazen Foundation, 1948.

Thom, D. A. *Everyday Problems of the Everyday Child.* New York: Appleton, 1927.

————. *Guiding the Adolescent.* Washington, D.C.: U.S. Government Printing Office, 1933.

————. *Normal Youth and Its Everyday Problems.* New York: Appleton, 1932.

Thomas, W. I. and Znaniecki, F. *The Polish Peasant.* Chicago: University of Chicago Press, 1918-1920.

Thorndike, E. L. *The Original Nature of Man.* New York: Teachers College, 1919.

—————. *The Psychology of Learning.* New York: Teachers College, 1913.

White, W. A. *The Mechanisms of Character.* New York: Macmillan, 1916.

Wieman, H. N. *Methods of Private Religious Living.* Macmillan, 1929.

—————. *The Source of Human Good.* Chicago: University of Chicago Press, 1946.

PART THREE

Chapter X

Anderson, John E. "The Development of Social Behavior," *The American Journal of Sociology,* May, 1939, pp. 839-54.

Bacmeister, R. W. *Growing Together.* New York: Appleton, 1947.

Biber, Barbara and others. *Child Life in School.* New York: E. P. Dutton & Co., 1942.

Bossard, James H. S. *The Sociology of Child Development.* New York: Harpers, 1948.

Bower, W. C. *Religion and the Good Life.* New York: Abingdon, 1933.

Counts, G. S. *Education and the Promise of America.* New York: Macmillan, 1946.

Coyle, Grace L. *Group Work with American Youth.* New York: Harpers, 1948.

Davis, Allison. "Socialization and Adolescent Behavior," *Readings in Social Psychology.* New York: Henry Holt & Co., 1947.

Edwards, Newton. *The School in the American Social Order.* Boston: Houghton Mifflin, 1947.

Elliott, H. S. *The Process of Group Thinking.* New York: Association Press, 1942.

Elsbree, Willard S. *The American Teacher: Evolution of Profession in a Democracy.* New York: American Book Co., 1939.

Fisk, Robert E. *Public Understanding of What Good Schools Can Do*. New York: Teachers College, 1945.

Gesell, A. L. and others. *The Child from Five to Ten*. New York: Harpers, 1946.

Gillin, J. L. and Gillin, P. *An Introduction to Sociology*. New York: Macmillan, 1945.

Jennings, Helen H. *Sociometry in Group Relations*. Washington, D.C.: American Council on Education, 1948.

Jersild, Arthur T. *Child Psychology*. New York: Prentice-Hall, 1947.

Lewin, Kurt. "Group Decision and Social Chance," *Readings in Social Psychology*. New York: Henry Holt & Co., 1947.

—————. *Resolving Social Conflicts*. New York: Harpers, 1948.

Mead, G. H. *Mind, Self, and Society*. Chicago: University of Chicago Press, 1934.

Murphey, Gardner, Murphey, Lois B., and Newcomb, Theodore M. *Experimental Social Psychology*. New York: Harpers, 1931.

Murphey, Lois B. "Social Factors in Child Development," *Readings in Social Psychology*. New York: Henry Holt & Co., 1947.

Newlon, Jesse. *Educational Administration as a Social Policy*. New York: Charles Scribner's Sons, 1934.

Olsen, Edward G. *School and Community Programs*. New York: Prentice-Hall, 1949.

Perry, R. B. *General Theory of Value*. New York: Longmans, Green & Co., 1926.

Piaget, Jean. "Social Factors in Moral Development," *Readings in Social Psychology*. New York: Henry Holt & Co., 1947.

Reavis, W. C. and Judd, Charles H. *The Teacher and Educational Administration*. Boston: Houghton Mifflin, 1942.

Sanders, Irwin T. "Getting Used to School," *Parents' Magazine*. November, 1942.

Sherif, Muzafer. *The Psychology of Social Norms*. New York: Harpers, 1936.

Chapter XI

Arbuthnot, May H. *Children and Books*. Chicago: Scott, Foresman & Co., 1947.

Carmichael, A. M. *Moral Situations of Six-Year-Olds as a Basis for Curriculum Construction.* Iowa City: University of Iowa Studies, 1927.

Dawson, Mildred A. *Language Teaching: Grades I and II.* New York: World Book Co., 1949.

An Experience Curriculum in English. New York: Appleton-Century, 1935.

Glaser, Emma. *On the Teaching of Junior High School English.* Cambridge, Mass.: Harvard University Press, 1945.

Hopkins, L. Thomas. *Interaction: The Democratic Process.* Boston: D. C. Heath & Co., 1941.

Jenkins, G. G., Schachter, Helen and Bauer, W. W. *These Are Your Children.* Chicago: Scott, Foresman & Co., 1949.

"Mathematics and Efficiency," *School Science and Mathematics,* Vol. XV, pp. 233-45.

"Mathematics and Life: The Vitalizing of Secondary Mathematics," *Social Science and Mathematics,* Vol. XV, pp. 105-15.

Mearns, Hughes. *Creative Youth.* Garden City, N.Y.: Doubleday, Page & Co., 1926.

Old, Mary E. *Give Us This Day.* Chicago: Allyn and Harpers, 1944.

Powdermaker, Hortense. *Probing Our Prejudices.* New York: Bacon, 1949.

Schwell, Hildred. *A Study of Boys and Girls.* Washington, D.C.: Delta Kappa Gamma Society, 1947.

Smith, David. *The Teaching of Junior High School.* New York: Macmillan, 1935.

Starbuck, E. D. and Shuttleworth, K. K. *A Guide to Literature for Character Education.* New York: Macmillan, 1930.

Stratemeyer, F. B., Forkner, H. L. and McKim, M. C. *Developing a Curriculum for Modern Living.* New York: Teachers College, 1947.

"Toward a New Curriculum," Washington, D.C.: Department of Supervision and Curriculum Development of the N.E.A., 1949 Yearbook.

"Using What We Know About Children in Developing Language Arts," *Childhood Education,* November, 1949.

Wrightstone, J. W. and Campbell, D. S. *Social Studies in the American Way of Life.* New York: Row, Peterson & Co., 1942.

Bulletins

Bulletin of the Association for Childhood Education.
Bulletin of the National Association of Secondary School
  Principals.
Kentucky Department of Education Bulletin.
Arkansas Elementary Schools Bulletin.
Cincinnati Public Schools Bulletin.
Fort Worth Public Schools Bulletin.
Grand Rapids Public Schools Bulletin.
Louisville Public Schools Curriculum Bulletin.

Chapter XII

Axline, V. M. *Play Therapy.* Atlanta: Houghton Mifflin,
  1947.
Baxter, Bernice. *Teacher-Pupil Relationships.* New York:
  Macmillan, 1941.
Block, Kathleen. *Manners for Moderns.* New York: Allyn &
  Bacon, 1941.
Cole, Luella. *Attaining Maturity.* New York: Rinehart & Co.,
  1944.
Detjen, Detjen. *Your High School Days.* New York: McGraw-
  Hill, 1947.
Fedder, Ruth. *A Girl Grows Up.* New York: McGraw-Hill,
  1948.
Forest, I. *Early Years at School.* New York: McGraw-Hill,
  1949.
Goodrich, Laurence. *Living with Others.* Cincinnati: Ameri-
  can Book Co., 1939.
Helping Teachers to Understand Children. Washington,
  D.C.: American Council on Education, 1915.
Hemming, James and Balls, Josephine. *The Child Is Right.*
  London: Longmans, Green & Co., 1947.
Hogue, Helen. *Bringing Up Ourselves.* New York: Charles
  Scribner's Sons, 1943.
Jenkins, G. G., Schachter, Helen and Bauer, W. W. *These
  Are Your Children.* Chicago: Scott, Foresman & Co., 1949.
Mackenzie, Catherine. *Parent and Child.* New York: Wil-
  liam Sloan Association, Inc., 1949.
Mental Health in Our Schools. Washington, D.C.: National
  Education Association, 1948.

National Forum, Inc., Guidance Series. Chicago:
  High School Life.
  Toward Adult Living.
  Discovering Myself.
  Being Teen-Agers.
  Planning My Future.
  About Growing Up.
Pierce, William G. *Youth Comes of Age.* New York: McGraw-Hill, 1948.
Pratt, C. *I Learn from Children.* New York: Simon & Shuster, 1939.
"The Quiet One," *Peabody Journal,* May, 1950.
Reynolds, Martha M. *Children from Seed to Sapling.* New York: McGraw-Hill, 1939.
Science Research Association Series, Chicago:
  Choosing Your Career.
  Getting Along with Others.
  How to Get a Job.
  Dating Days.
  Growing Up Socially.
  How to Live with Parents.
Smart, M. S., and Smart, R. C. *Living and Learning with Children.* Boston: Houghton Mifflin, 1949.
Strain, F. B. *Teen Days.* New York: Appleton-Century, 1946.
Torgerson, T. L. *Studying Children.* New York: Dryden Press, 1947.
Truancy. Lancaster, Pa.: National Committee for Mental Hygiene, Inc., April, 1950.
Sources of Films
  Information regarding available films may be secured from the Bureau of Audio-Visual Materials, University of Kentucky Department of Extension.

Chapter XIII

"Administrators' Function in Redirecting Physical Education," *American School Board Journal,* April, 1945.
"Athletics and Recreation," *Athletic Journal,* February, 1948.
Bowers, Ethel. *Recreation.* New York: A. S. Brown & Co., 1934.
Broody, Lois P. *Health and Physical Education for Small*

Schools. Lincoln, Neb.: University of Nebraska Press, 1942.

Brown, F. J. *Educational Sociology.* New York: Prentice-Hall, Inc., 1947.

"Camping as an Opportunity for Providing Real Experiences," unpublished paper, University of Kentucky Library.

"Can Character be Developed?" *Scholastic Coach,* June, 1948.

"Character Training in Athletics," *Scholastic Coach,* March, 1942.

"Childhood and the Democratic Future," *Journal of the National Education Association,* December, 1948.

"Dancing in the Dark," *Hygeia,* July, 1944.

Davis, J. E. *Play and Mental Health.* New York: A. S. Brown & Co., 1938.

Ellson, Hal. *Duke.* New York: C. Scribner's Sons, 1949.

Harbin, E. O. *The Fun Encyclopedia.* New York: Abingdon-Cokesbury, 1940.

"Human Engineering through Industrial Recreation," *Athletic Journal,* March, 1943.

"Interschool Sports and the Educational Program," *Athletic Journal,* September, 1936.

"Juvenile Delinquency and the Schools," *National Society for the Study of Education Yearbook,* 1948.

LaSalle, Dorothy. *Guidance of Children through Physical Education.* New York: A. S. Barnes & Co., 1937.

Lee, Mable. *The Conduct of Physical Education.* New York: A. S. Barnes & Co., 1937.

Mason, B. S. and Mitchell, E. D. *Active Games and Contests.* New York: A. S. Barnes & Co., 1938.

Meyer, H. D. and Brightbill, C. K. *Community Recreation: A Guide to Its Organization and Administration.* Boston: D. C. Heath, 1948.

"Morale Makes Winners," *Athletic Journal,* October, 1945.

Neilson, N. P. and Van Hagen, W. *Physical Education for Elementary Schools.* New York: A. S. Barnes & Co., 1930.

Neumeyer, M. H. and Neumeyer, F. S. *Leisure and Recreation.* New York: A. S. Barnes & Co., 1936.

Nixon, E. W. and Cozens, F. W. *An Introduction to Physical Education.* Philadelphia: W. B. Saunders & Co., 1947.

O'Keefe, Ruth and Fahey, Helen. *Physical Education and Recreation for Elementary Grades.* St. Louis: C. V. Mosby Co., 1949.

Patty, W. W. *Teaching Health and Safety in Elementary Grades.* New York: Prentice-Hall, 1940.

"Philosophical Interpretation of a Program of Physical Education in a Teachers College," *Physical Education and Recreation,* December, 1944.

"Physical Education and Directed Recreation," *School Elementary and Secondary Education,* February, 1944.

"Physical Education Does Educate," *American Association of College Registrars Journal,* October, 1944.

"Physical Education Stimulates Mental Activity," *Training School Bulletin,* December, 1945.

"Physical Education, the Stepchild, Should be Adopted," *American School Bulletin,* February, 1945.

Reynolds, Martha M. *Children from Seed to Sapling.* New York: McGraw-Hill, 1939.

Salt, E. B. and others. *Teaching Physical Education in the Elementary School.* New York: A. S. Barnes & Co., 1942.

Sehon, E. L. and others. *Physical Education Methods for Elementary Schools.* Philadelphia: W. B. Saunders & Co., 1948.

Sharman, Jackson R. *The Teaching of Physical Education.* New York: A. S. Barnes & Co., 1936.

Slavson, S. R. *Recreation and the Total Personality.* New York: Association Press, 1946.

"Some Contributions of Physical Education to an Educated Life," *Journal of Health and Public Education,* January, 1949.

Staley, S. C. *The New Curriculum in Physical Education.* New York: A. S. Barnes & Co., 1939.

"Technical and Emotional Obstacles Which Confront the Physical Educator," *Journal of Health and Public Education,* January, 1949.

Understanding Delinquency. Washington, D.C.: Federal Security Administration, 1949.

"Value of Squad Activities," *Secondary Education,* October, 1945.

"What Can Physical Education Contribute to World Peace?" *Health and Public Education,* May, 1945.

"You Can't Beat Spirit," *Athletic Journal,* November, 1943.

Films

"Your Child is a Genius."

"Leaders for Leisure."

"One Thousand Dollars for Recreation."

"Playtown, U.S.A."

For information regarding speakers, advice, or other assistance, address:

State Department of Parks, Frankfort, Ky., Miss Lucy Smith, Director.

State Division of Game and Fish, Frankfort, Ky., Ed Adams, Director, Junior Conservation Program.

Department of Physical Education, University of Kentucky.

Chapter XIV

Ames, E. S. *Religion,* Chap. VII, "Religion and Art." New York: Holt, 1929.

Ames, Van Meter. *Aesthetics of the Novel.* Chicago: University of Chicago Press, 1928.

Bernard, L. L. *Introduction to Social Psychology,* index on "Symbols." New York: Holt, 1936.

Bower, W. C. *The Church at Work in the Modern World,* Chap. IV, "Religious Ceremonials and Their Symbolism," by E. S. Ames. Chicago: University of Chicago Press, 1935.

Coit, Stanton. *Social Worship.* New York: Macmillan, 1913.

Craven, Thomas. *Men of Art.* New York: Simon and Shuster, 1931.

Dewey, John. *Art as Experience.* New York: Minton, Balch & Co., 1934.

Harrison, Jane. *Ancient Art and Ritual.* New York: H. Holt and Co., 1913.

Meland, B. E. *Modern Man's Worship.* New York: Harpers, 1934.

Reinach, S. *Apollo.* New York: Charles Scribner's Sons, 1907.

Ruskin, John. *Modern Painters.* London: J. M. Dent & Co., 1906.

Sperry, W. L. *Reality in Worship.* New York: Macmillan, 1925.

Taine, Hippolyte Adolphe. *Philosophy of Art.* London: H. Ballière, 1865.

Tolstoy, Lyof N. *What Is Art?* New York: Thomas Y. Crowell & Co., 1899.

Vogt, Von Ogden. *Art and Religion.* New Haven: Yale University Press, 1921.

Wieman, H. N. *Methods of Private Religious Living.* New York: Macmillan, 1928.

Appendix

A POLICY FOR CO-OPERATION WITH COMMUNITY AGENCIES

Since the text of this volume was written, the program therein described and interpreted, in moving into its second phase of expansion, as an aspect of that development has undertaken to formulate a policy of co-operation with other community agencies. The following Appendix is a statement of that policy.

I

BASIC CONSIDERATIONS

Since moral and spiritual values come into being in and are conditioned by the experience of the whole self in interaction with its total environment, it follows that anything that influences the experience of the pupil anywhere must be of deep concern to the public school. The pupil's experience transcends the boundaries of all the institutions and groups of which he is a member. The cultivation of moral and spiritual values in the young of the community is an undertaking that no single agency working alone or many agencies working independently with their own objectives and programs can hope to accomplish. This means that a school that seeks to discover and develop moral and spiritual values in the public education of children and young people must seek to establish understandings and effective co-operation with all the constructive agencies of the community that in one way or another influence their attitudes and behavior. In such an undertaking the constructive agencies of the community need to become what the Educational Policies Commission has appropriately called "partners" in a common responsibility.

Such understandings and co-operation involve all the constructive agencies of the community—the school, the family, the churches, the social agencies, the press, and radio and television. All of these because of the experiences which they provide affect, either positively or negatively, the moral and spiritual standards and behaviors of growing persons.

Most communities present another problem of a deeply significant and difficult nature. This problem arises from the presence of destructive agencies that exert an influence in conflict with the efforts of the school to build moral and spiritual ideals. Among these are taverns, roadhouses, unsupervised dance halls, organized gambling that has brought dishonor upon athletics, and the agencies that lure high-school young people into drug addiction or sexual debauchery. There is urgent need that public opinion be aroused to bring these influences that hinder or destroy human personality under control, either by eliminating them or rendering them ineffective. This negative task is one that no agency working alone or independently of others can accomplish.

The institution that by its nature, prestige, and resources is best fitted to assume the initiative in securing the co-operation of community agencies will depend upon the conditions prevailing in each given community. But in most communities the school, because it is the public agency of all the people, is supported by public funds, and reaches all the children and young people of school age except those in parochial schools, is best equipped to take the initiative in securing the co-operation of community agencies.

If the school assumes the initiative in co-operation, however, it should not invade the structures and functions of other community agencies, but should respect and protect their prerogatives and autonomy, as, for example, in its demands upon the pupil's time, energy, and interests. On the other hand, the school should resist the encroachments of other institutions upon its prerogatives as, for example, in the case of the efforts of special interest groups to bring pressure to bear upon the schools or to exploit them, or of the attempt of sectarian churches to teach religion in the schools or to divert public school funds to ecclesiastical use. The Kentucky Movement of Moral and Spiritual Values in Education unalterably is committed to the strict separation of church and state and unequivocally is opposed to teaching religion in the public schools in any functional co-operation with the churches or their clergy. In the same way the school should respect and protect the rights and responsibilities of parents within the provisions of the law regarding discipline, a reasonable distribution of the child's time and activities, and the determination of the child's religious and political beliefs.

It should be recognized, however, that in a dynamic society the determination of functions and structural boundaries among institutions cannot be rigid or static, as is evidenced by the fact that in recent years the family, the church, and the local community have been giving off functions to industry, to the state, and to the school as a state institution. Nevertheless, if these basic historic social institutions are to preserve their integrity, this tendency toward a redistribution of functions should be appraised critically and brought under conscious and intentional control rather than be allowed to drift. As of this stage in our culture, it would seem better for the school to err on the side of preserving and supporting the integrity of these institutions rather than contribute to their disintegration. In the meantime, in order to meet the needs of children and young people, a safe and proper rule to follow is for the school to take over the functions of other institutions only when it is clear that through lack of initiative or resources they have proven themselves incapable of performing these functions.

In many communities in the nation a Community Council already exists, having come into being to provide just such co-operation of community agencies in the interest of child and youth needs. Where such a Council exists, the school should work through it. If the Council is effective, the school should adopt toward it the same policy as in its own program—that of *emphasis upon moral and spiritual values.* Where the Community Council is ineffective the school should seek to make it effective before creating a new agency.

II

PROCEDURES

A Conference of Community Agencies

The first step in co-operation may well be the holding of a series of joint conferences of school personnel, parents, religious leaders, social workers, representatives of civic clubs, and persons working with juvenile delinquents. The purpose of such conferences would be:

A. To study the entire range of the experience of children and young people in the interaction of whole persons with their total environment.

B. To list the areas of need that are being met satisfactorily by the several agencies and the areas that are being neglected or are only partially met.

C. To list the specific resources of the several agencies for meeting these needs.

D. To agree upon the allocation of primary responsibility for meeting child and youth needs in a shared total responsibility.

Where an effective Community Council exists, this may be done through the Council.

Things in General That the School May Provide

A. An actual experience of moral and spiritual values in their functional relation to life in the school community and the learning process, as these values are contained in the great cultural traditions.

B. Assistance to the child in understanding and appraising his experience in the school and beyond the school in the Great Society.

C. The development of the capacity and disposition critically to appraise the many divergent and often conflicting behaviors and standards of life in the school and the community, together with criteria by which to judge and improve them, as in the case of taste in the selection of book and magazine reading, movies, radio and television programs, and recreation.

D. An understanding and appreciation of the nature and function of social institutions, such as the home, the school, the churches, the social agencies, the processes of production and distribution, and the media of communication as these are related to each other in the total life of the community, so that the child will have a realistic sense of the community as a collective functioning whole and of the relation of the several institutions to community needs.

E. Counseling to pupils in meeting their problems.

The School and the Family

The family is the oldest and in many ways still the most fundamental educational agency. Through it the child inherits the capacities of original nature and the basic patterns of personality. In it the child has his first experience with his environing natural and social world. Through it the child inherits in the beginning his cultural heritage and absorbs its general patterns and value systems. In it he is conditioned organically and emotionally to behavior patterns that are likely to persist throughout his life. Many of his behavior maladjustments that come to light in the school have their origin in tensions and maladjustments in his home life. Next to the family, the school is responsible for the largest block of his time and energy. It is, therefore, of the utmost importance that the school and the family establish and maintain intimate relations of understanding and co-operation.

A. Things the school may do:

1. Give the child an understanding of the nature and function of the family in society.

2. Create appreciation of, respect for, and loyalty to the family.

3. Prepare in terms of what the school has to offer for homemaking and parenthood.

4. Provide knowledge of family finance, including especially the arrangement of the family budget.

5. Train in home arrangement, furniture design, and decoration.

6. Establish means of continuous communication regarding content of courses and the school program.

7. Visit homes of pupils for the purpose of establishing rapport, friendly personal relations, and an understanding of the home environment of the pupil.

8. Create occasions for the visitation of the school by parents.

9. In the interest of the child, create understanding and appreciation on the part of the parents about what the school is attempting to do in the cultivation of moral and spiritual values and enlist their co-operation.

B. What the family may do:

1. Provide the school with information regarding the child's backgrounds, personality traits, interests, out-of-school activities, health, handicaps, and so on.

2. Inform the school regarding any tensions or maladjustments or frustrations that have been occasioned by the child's school experience.

3. Provide assistance in the counseling of the individual child regarding personal adjustments or behavior problems.

4. Co-operate in guiding the individual child at the secondary level in arriving at a choice of a vocation and in working out a prevocational program of study and in the choice of a college or technical school.

5. Provide the child with a wholesome atmosphere of affection and security for the growth of wholesome personality and the achievement of moral and spiritual ideals.

6. Consult directly with teachers as questions are raised by the children and problems arise in connection with the program of the school.

Fortunately, for such clearance and co-operation the Parent-Teacher Association provides a most effective means of mutual understanding and effort.

The School and the Churches

While the fundamental principles of the Movement do not permit the teaching of religion in the public schools by the churches, there are many ways in which the school and the churches may co-operate as separate and distinct institutions to their mutual advantage in the cultivation of moral and spiritual values. This is especially so since the special concern of the churches is with moral and spiritual values. In accepting its responsibility for the discovery and development of moral and spiritual values under the conditions imposed by the school as a state institution and with such resources as it possesses, the school's Program of Moral and Spiritual Values in Education is in no sense in competition with or a substitute for religious education as carried on by the churches in terms of their several theological or ecclesiastical interpretations, nor does it relieve them of their full responsibility in this field. In the shared responsibility of meeting the needs of children and of society, there are certain things that the school is best equipped to do, while at the same time there are other things that the churches can best do. In such a division of responsibility there are many areas of co-operation where each may further what the other is doing.

A. What the school may do:

1. Provide the child with the actual experience of moral and spiritual values as they arise and function in the manifold experiences of the school community and in relation to the cultural heritage, but without theological interpretation.

2. Give an understanding of the relation of religion as a valuational experience to culture and of the influence of a changing culture upon the historical expressions of religion.

3. Through an understanding of the differences of theological and ecclesiastical expressions of religion and the historical conditions under which they have arisen, develop respect for different religious beliefs and practices and tolerance toward those who hold and practice them.

4. Through organized visitations, observe the forms of organized religion in the community, noting such items as architecture, budgets, membership, distinctive beliefs, forms of worship, organization, and the place of religion in the life of the community.

5. Avoid as far as possible destructive conflicts between the scientific subjects and traditional theological beliefs by sympathetically helping the pupil to face them objectively in a constructive spirit of inquiry and by directing him to his pastor or parents for guidance concerning the problem involved. The school should seek to conserve essential religious convictions and not to destroy them, remembering that persons live by their convictions and that irreparable damage will be done by allowing old convictions to disintegrate without helping replace them by equally convincing ones.

6. Formally or informally on the secondary level take account of religion objectively as a phenomenon of culture as it manifests itself in literature, history, institutions, social behavior, and the development of ideas, but without theological interpretation. This should be done with complete impartiality to all historical and contemporary religious communions and religious beliefs and practices and without the teacher expressing personal bias toward any particular faith or seeking in any way to influence the

beliefs and loyalties of pupils. This lays upon the teacher in the public schools the grave ethical responsibility of being on guard against identifying the religious beliefs and practices of his own communion with religion as a historical and cultural phenomenon or against comparing or contrasting his own beliefs with those of others.

7. By dealing with religion in its functional and universal aspects as a phenomenon of culture, lay the basic foundation of understanding and appreciation upon which the churches may build what they deem necessary or desirable in the further cultivation of religious beliefs and attitudes in terms of their several theological or ecclesiastical traditions.

B. What the churches may do:

1. Through the characteristic historical language of religion—creed, symbol, ritual, ordinances, gesture—make moral and spiritual values explicit and articulate in terms of the theological presuppositions of the respective communion or faith.

2. Where such is deemed necessary, provide the sanctions of a supernatural or ecclesiastical authority.

3. Provide a sustained and sustaining fellowship devoted to the cultivation of religious ideals, not only in the intimate face-to-face local church group, but in a universal contemporary ecumenical fellowship and in a centuries-old continuing religious community.

4. Provide the means for the systematic cultivation of the religious life through prayer, meditation, self-examination, rededication, the use of the ordinances, and corporate worship.

5. Provide opportunities for developing loyalties to religious leaders and causes and wholehearted participation in specific religious enterprises such as missions, social justice, world brotherhood, and peace.

6. Prepare the pupil for resolving creatively the apparent conflict between science and religion and provide sympathetic and patient guidance in dealing with his religious perplexities.

The School and the Social Agencies

The foregoing analyses of the possibilities of co-operation between the school and the family and the school and the churches may serve as illustrations of possible ways of co-operation between the school and the several social agencies, such as the Family Service Agency and the various forms of relief, public health, recreational, and youth organizations.

The purpose of this statement of policy in the field of co-operation is not to offer a blueprint of procedure, but to outline certain basic principles and to suggest possible ways by which local schools, operating under the specific and unique situations in their own communities, may pool their resources with those of other agencies in an attempt to meet the needs of the child and youth population of the community. Co-operation is more a matter of attitude and spirit than of formal technique. Granted the will to work together without pressure, in understanding, and with a common purpose, the problem is to create and maintain channels of communication, to eliminate waste through duplication of programs and effort, and to provide for the neglected areas of child and youth needs.

Index

Curriculum Content: analysis of, general values in curriculum, 129-130; the humanities, 131-135; social sciences, 135-137; natural sciences, 137-138; mathematics, 138-139; vocational exploratory areas, 140-141; physical education, 141-142

Desire: relation to value, 64-66; source of motivation, 66-67
Developing situations: illustrations from counseling, 103-109; illustrations from curriculum content, 99-103; illustrations from school community, 94-99; illustrations from sports and recreation, 109-112; illustrations from symbolic expression, 112-116; psychological basis of, 52-58; steps involved in, 93
Dewey, John, 56, 67, 77
Dimock, H. S., 69
Donovan, H. L., 22

Eastern Kentucky State College, 22
Education: as concerned with growth of whole persons, 47, 73; as creative experience, 64; as discipline, 41; devaluation of, 3-7; shift of from teaching to learning, 41; trend toward integration of, 86-87
Educational Policies Commission, 12-13, 185
Educational situation: problem of moral and spiritual values in American education, 3-13; toward a solution of the problem, 14-25
Effort, relation of to values, 66
Emotions, 67
Experience: bipolar, 48; creative, 57, 59, 64; control of, 58-60; cuts across all institutions, 199; integration of, 70-73; interaction between self and objective world, 48-52, 58-59; personality outgrowth of, 47-48; religious quality of, 72-73; source of, 48-52; structure of, 53-58; tends to fall apart, 70-71

Family, the: oldest and most fundamental educational agency, 203; things it may do in developing moral and spiritual values, 203-204
Foreign language, 132
Four-H Clubs, 17
Froebel, F., 50, 152
Functional relation of values to experience: to be real must be experienced, 61-64; psychological situation in which values arise, 64-68; social participation as source of, 68; conflicts in, 70
Future Farmers of America, 17
Future Homemakers of America, 17

Gildersleeve, B. L., 54
Girl Scouts, 17
God, 77

Habit, 55
Harper, W. R., 16
Hartshorne, Hugh, 69-70
Harvard University, 86
Health education, 141-142
Herbart, J. F., 41

Index